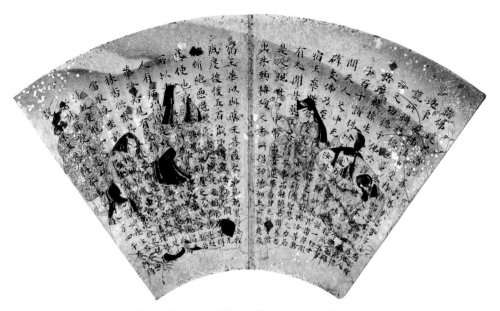

Plate 1. *Fan-shaped Album of the Lotus Sutra* (*Senmen Hokkekyō sasshi*), twelfth century. Shitennōji Temple.

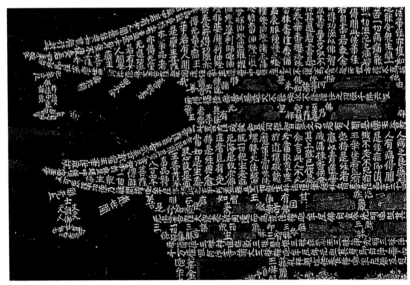

Plate 2. *Jeweled Stupa Mandala in Gold Script* (*Konji hōtō mandara*) (detail),
twelfth to thirteenth century. Myōhōji Temple. Image: Sakai City Museum.

Plate 3. Himeji Castle.

Opposite page:
Plate 4. *Kasuga Mandala* (*Kasuga mandara*),
thirteenth century. Tokyo National Museum.

Plate 5. Garden outside Hōjō residence, Daisen'in, Daitokuji Temple.
Photograph © Mizuno Katsuhiko.

Plate 7. Hishida Shunsō, *Landscape of the Four Seasons* (*Shiki sansui*) (detail),
1910. National Museum of Modern Art, Tokyo.

Plate 6. Sesshū, *Landscapes of the Four Seasons*
(*Shiki sansui-zu*) (detail), 1486. Mōri Museum.

Plate 8. Tawaraya Sōtatsu (painting), Hon'ami Kōetsu (calligraphy),
Crane Scroll (*Tsuru shita-e wakakan*), seventeenth century.
Kyoto National Museum.

Plate 10. Ogata Kōrin, *Irises at Yatsuhashi (Eight Bridges)* (*Yatsuhashi-zu byōbu*),
ca. 1710. Metropolitan Museum of Art.

Plate 9. "Hatsune" *Maki-e* Box (Hatsune maki-e tebako),
seventeenth century. Tokyo National Museum.
Image: TNM Image Archives.

Plate 11. Munakata Shikō, "Three Sisters" (San shimai no saku) from *Poems by Tanizaki Jun'ichirō* (*Utauta hanga-saku*), 1956. Ōhara Museum of Art.

Plate 12. Kuroda Seiki,
Reading (*Dokusho*),
1890–1891. Tokyo
National Museum.
Image: TNM Image Archives.

Plate 13. Kitagawa Utamaro,
*Naniwa Okita Admiring Herself in a
Mirror* (*Sugatami shichinin keshō*).
Metropolitan Museum of Art.

Plate 14. Kanō Eitoku, *Scenes In and Around Kyoto* (*Rakuchū rakugai-zu byōbu*)—Uesugi screens, Muromachi period. Yonezawa City Uesugi Museum.
Top: right screen
Bottom: left screen

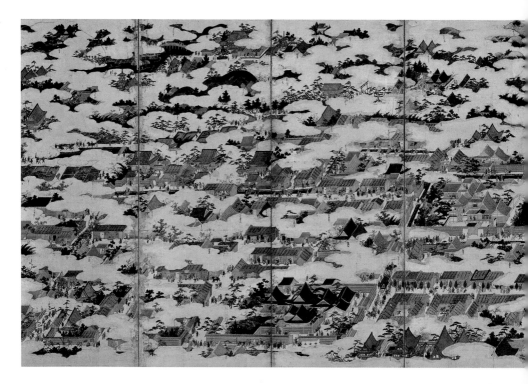

Plate 15. Tawaraya Sōtatsu, *Bugaku Dancers* (*Bugaku-zu byōbu*),
seventeenth century. Daigoji Temple.

Plate 16. Takahashi Yuichi, *Sea Bream* (*Tai*), 1879. Kotohiragū Shrine.

Plate 17. Utagawa Hiroshige, "Plum Estate, Kameido" (Kameido Umeyashiki) from *One Hundred Famous Views of Edo* (*Meisho Edo hyakkei*), 1857. National Diet Library.

Plate 18. Vincent van Gogh, *Flowering Plum Orchard (after Hiroshige)* (*Bloeiende pruimenboomgaard [naar Hiroshige]*), 1887. Van Gogh Museum, Amsterdam (Vincent van Gogh Foundation).

Plate 19. Yokoyama Taikan, *A Day in the Pacific Ocean* (*Aru hi no taiheiyō*), 1952. National Museum of Modern Art, Tokyo.

Plate 20. Hieronymus Bosch,
The Garden of Earthly Delights
(right panel, detail), 1490–1510.
Museo Nacional del Prado.
© Photographic Archive
Museo Nacional del Prado.

Plate 21. *Demons' Night Parade Picture-Scroll* (*Hyakki yagyō emaki*) (details), Edo period.
International Research Center for Japanese Studies.

THE JAPANESE SENSE OF BEAUTY

JAPAN LIBRARY

THE JAPANESE SENSE OF BEAUTY

Takashina Shūji

Translated by Matt Treyvaud

Japan Publishing Industry Foundation for Culture

Note to the reader: For Japanese words, long vowels are indicated by macrons, except in familiar place names. Japanese and Chinese names are written family name first as is customary in East Asia.

Japanese Historical Periods

ca. 10,000 BCE	Jōmon	1333–1573	Muromachi
ca. 300 BCE	Yayoi	1573–1600	Azuchi-Momoyama
ca. 300–592	Kofun	1600–1868	Edo
592–710	Asuka	1868–1912	Meiji
710–794	Nara	1912–1926	Taishō
794–1185	Heian	1926–1989	Shōwa
1185–1333	Kamakura	1989–present	Heisei

The Japanese Sense of Beauty
Takashina Shūji. Translated by Matt Treyvaud.

Published by Japan Publishing Industry Foundation for Culture (JPIC)
3-12-3 Kanda-Jinbocho, Chiyoda-ku, Tokyo 101-0051, Japan.

© Takashina Shūji, 2015

First English edition: March 2018

English translation © Japan Publishing Industry Foundation for Culture, 2018

Originally published in Japanese under the title of *Nihonjin ni totte utsukushisa to wa nanika* by Chikumashobo Ltd., in 2015.

English publishing rights arranged with Chikumashobo Ltd.

Book design: Point & Line Co., Ltd.
Jacket and cover illustration: Ogata Kōrin, *Irises* (right screen, detail), eighteenth century. Nezu Museum.

As this book is published primarily to be donated to overseas universities, research institutions, public libraries and other organizations, commercial publication rights are available. For all enquiries regarding those rights, please contact the publisher of the original Japanese edition at the following address:
Foreign Rights, Chikumashobo Ltd., 2-5-3, Kuramae, Taitō-ku, Tokyo 111-8755, Japan.

All rights reserved. Printed in Japan.
ISBN 978-4-86658-020-3
http://www.jpic.or.jp/japanlibrary/

Contents

I. Word and Image: The Japanese Aesthetic Consciousness   29

The *Kokin Wakashū* and Japanese Aesthetics

The Significance of Imperial *Waka* Anthologies

Crossing the Word—Image Border

Sori: A Plastic Sensitivity

European Curves, Japanese *Sori*

The Plasticity of Hiragana

Comparing Japanese and Western Architecture

What Is a Torii?

Closeness to Nature in Japanese Aesthetics

The Four Seasons in Japanese Painting

Emoji, *Moji-e*, and Play

Word and Image Together

Chirashigaki and *Kaeshigaki*

The Uniqueness of Chinese Characters in Japan

Word and Image in Handcraft Design

Fujiwara no Teika's Aesthetics of Rejection

Ariwara no Narihira's "Eight Bridges"

II. Japanese Beauty, Western Beauty   87

III. Roots of the Japanese Aesthetic Consciousness   147

Preface to the English Edition

In the early twentieth century, the Japanese writer Natsume Sōseki spent two years in London studying English literature. He later drew on this experience in his *Theory of Literature*, where he wrote:

> My invitations to go snow-viewing provoked laughter there. On one occasion my claim that the moon had a deep pathos was met with astonishment.

To the Japanese, snow, the moon, and the like are not mere natural phenomena. They are an intimate and deeply felt presence in our daily emotional lives and expressions of sentiment—"friends of the soul" that have inspired countless poems over the centuries. Sōseki may have had one of these poems in mind when he invited his English acquaintances to go snow-viewing—perhaps the famous haiku by Bashō:

iza saraba	now then, let's away
yukimi ni korobu	to view the snow until
tokoro made	we tumble over

But the response Sōseki received was entirely different, leading him to realize that the Japanese love of nature is particularly strong. This Japanese sense of beauty is reflected not only in everyday Japanese attitudes and behavior but even in moral codes and value systems.

This book is a collection of texts exploring the unique characteristics of this sense of beauty, largely by comparison with the West. It is my sincere hope that the chapters that follow may provide some assistance to promoting the understanding of Japanese culture more broadly.

Takashina Shūji

Preface to the Japanese Edition

I was on the Shinkansen to Kyoto once with a friend visiting from France. It was a fine day, but the mist around Mount Fuji was so thick that it obscured the mountain entirely. My friend, who was visiting Japan for the first time, jokingly suggested that perhaps there *was* no Mount Fuji after all.

"Oh, no," I replied at once. "She's just very capricious."

My friend looked very surprised. "Mount Fuji is female?" he asked.

That was when I realized for the first time that, in French, *Mont Fuji*, like *Mont Blanc* and *Mont San-Michel*, takes the masculine gender. When I speak French, I naturally treat *Mont Fuji* as a masculine noun as well, but apparently I still tended to envisage the mountain itself as a graceful and elegant lady.

Sengen Shrine, in the foothills of Mount Fuji, was originally dedicated to the mountain itself, which was viewed as a goddess. It eventually became a center of worship of the female deity Konohanasakuya-hime in ceremonies still performed today. Mount Fuji also plays a key role in the tale of the moon princess Kaguya-hime, and the legend of the celestial maiden with her feathered mantle (*hagoromo*). No doubt all of this helped form my impression of Mount Fuji as feminine. Certainly, among the many paintings of Mount Fuji, there is no shortage of works pairing the mountain with a gracefully dancing divine beauty.

But things are different in Europe. Since ancient Greece, mountain deities in the West have been imagined as male, like thunder, wind, and river gods. In paintings, they are almost always enormous, muscular men. Coming from this cultural background, it is no wonder that my friend was surprised to hear me call Mount Fuji "she."

We cannot look directly on our own face; only by looking in a mirror can begin to grasp what makes us unique. The image in the mirror is us, but at the same time it is how we are seen by others outside ourselves. When considering forms of creative expression like arts (architecture, painting, crafts) and literature (stories, poetry, theater), adopting the perspective of a foreign culture—such as the West, in Japan's case—and comparing it with our own viewpoint can help clarify the unique characteristics of our own culture's artistic traditions.

The works collected in this volume add up to what might be called a treatise on Japanese culture as viewed through this sort of "compound perspective."

I

Word and Image:
The Japanese Aesthetic
Consciousness

Based on a speech given in Shizuoka Prefecture, 2014.

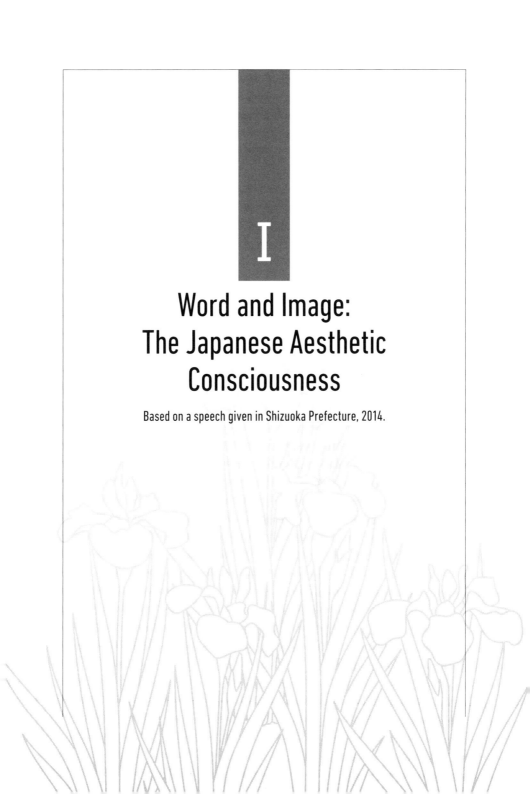

Word and Image:
The Japanese Aesthetic Consciousness

The poetic form known as *waka*, literally "Japanese song," has played a key role in Japanese literature since ancient times. A *waka* consists of five lines—strictly speaking, *ku* or "phrases"—in a 5-7-5-7-7 syllable pattern. Where paintings and other visual artworks are preserved as images, *waka* come down to us as words alone. Nevertheless, they share in an aesthetic consciousness found in all Japanese expressive works. This consciousness is a major part of Japanese tradition, influencing the thought, speech, and even behavioral patterns of Japan, and quite unlike anything found in the West.

Words and pictures are fundamentally different things. In the West, they have accordingly been considered two utterly distinct worlds, but in Japan connections between them have been made since ancient times. Today's Japanese children still play drawing games in which Japanese characters are written in a certain way to form a picture on the page. These are known as *moji-e*, "character-pictures." The *henohenomoheji* face, drawn using characters from the hiragana syllabary, dates back to the Edo period, and the tradition as a whole has an even longer history.

The opposite of *moji-e* is emoji, "picture-characters," which are popular among young people today. I do not use them myself, but my granddaughter often adds a smiling face or some other emoji at the end of an e-mail sent to one of her many friends: "Bye!", and then a smile. If she is angry, there are emoji for that too. In fact, the selection of emoji on today's cellphones is so wide that there are several "angry face" emoji: one very angry, one just a little cross, and so on. Rows and rows of emoji, waiting to be used. My granddaughter once told me there were over three hundred, and I understand that figure has increased today.

Similar ideas can be found outside Japan, of course, albeit in simpler form. T-shirts reading "I ♡ NY," where the heart is an emoji pronounced *love*, are one example. But among the younger generation in Japan, not only are emoji used in far greater volume, they are a completely unremarkable part of everyday life. This is something one does not see overseas.*

In Japan, interplay between word and image dates back to ancient times, and is visible even in works of art.

The *Kokin Wakashū* and Japanese Aesthetics

The *Kokin wakashū* is a tenth-century *waka* anthology. Its title literally means "Collection of Old and New *Waka*," but even in English it is usually referred to as the *Kokin wakashū* or just the *Kokinshū* for brevity. It has two prefaces, one written in classical Chinese and the other in Japanese. The Japanese preface, written using the *kana* syllabary and therefore usually called the "*kana* preface," is said to have been composed by Ki no Tsurayuki, chief editor of the *Kokinshū* and an accomplished poet himself. It begins as follows:

> Japanese poetry has the human heart as its seed and grows into myriad leaves of words. It is the expression of how people feel in their hearts about what they see and hear in this world full of words and deeds. The bush warbler singing in the flowers, the voice of the frog that lives in the river—hearing these, we must ask: what living thing does not recite poetry of its own? Effortlessly moving heaven and earth, arousing the sympathies of demons and gods invisible to the eye, calming relations between men and women, and soothing the warrior's heart: it is poetry that can do all these things.

This is arguably the first clear statement of the Japanese aesthetic con-

---

* Translator's note: The use of emoji outside Japan has, of course, increased considerably in recent years.

sciousness. More than just a preface to a book of poetry, it encapsulates the entire Japanese view of beauty. Let us consider it in more detail.

"Japanese poetry has the human heart as its seed …" The first two words, "Japanese poetry," correspond to *Yamato-uta* in the original. This literally means "Yamato poetry," Yamato being a poetic name for Japan at that point. In other words, this is another way of saying *waka*. The seed of *waka* is the human heart, and words are their flowering.

"It is the expression of how people feel in their hearts …" The same could be said of Japanese people today, who express the many things they think and feel in the 5-7-5-7-7 *waka* form, or as haiku in 5-7-5.

"The bush warbler …" Here Tsurayuki introduces the idea of poetry as a universal practice, on which more follows below.

The next part is about the uses of poetry. It seems quite natural to Japanese readers, but apparently not to Westerners. Donald Keene, who has been very influential in introducing the literature of Japan to the West, has written in his history of Japanese literature and elsewhere about the strong impression the *kana* preface made on him when he read it in his youth.

In my experience, two particular parts of this section raise Western eyebrows. The first is "what living thing does not recite poetry of its own?" In the English-speaking world, poets are a breed apart—recipients of special inspiration from God and bearers of a unique genius that other people lack. In Japan, however, anyone can be a poet. The eighth-century *Man'yōshū* anthology contains poems by *sakimori* or "frontier guards"—regular men conscripted to guard Japan's western coast. Even completely normal, everyday people like this wrote poetry.

I sometimes still encounter visitors to Japan who do not believe that poetry could be such a widespread pursuit. My response is to suggest that they buy a newspaper and see for themselves. Whichever paper they buy, I explain, they will find a daily poetry column running *waka* and haiku submitted by readers from all over the country—hundreds, if not thousands, of people from all walks of life. To someone from a country where few people write poems at all, this is astonishing.

"Effortlessly moving heaven and earth …" can be even more surprising to Western readers. In ancient times, the earth was thought to be fixed, with only the sun and moon in motion. Like rain and thunder, these were beyond humanity's control, leading observers to wonder what did have power over them. In the West, the ancient Greeks imagined special deities for this purpose; once Christianity became dominant, that role was assigned to God. There is a painting by Raphael—any visitor to the Vatican can see it right there on the ceiling—that shows God moving the entire celestial sphere. The Japanese idea that simply reciting a poem could move heaven and earth struck the youthful Professor Keene as simply absurd.

The legend of the ninth-century poet Ono no Komachi making rain with poetry is well known; true or false, those of my generation heard it often in our childhood. Then there was the opposite case—the poem written by the third Kamakura shogun Minamoto no Sanetomo when there was too *much* rain:

toki ni yori	at times it can
sugureba tami no	be too much and become
nageki nari	a woe to the people—
Hachi Dai-ryū-ō	Eight Great Dragon Kings
ame yametamae	I beg you, stop the rain

Sanetomo's recitation of this poem is said to have ended the rain. Poetry can not only move the earth, it can also control the weather. The *Kokinshū*'s *kana* preface says that it can also win over "demons and gods invisible to the eye," and the ancient Japanese used it for this purpose as a matter of course. According to Professor Keene, this is another great difference from the West.

Next comes "men and women." This is only to be expected; there are countless love poems among the anthologies surviving from ancient times. Next, "the warrior's heart": even soldiers wrote poetry, right up to the military dictators that were the shoguns, and we have countless examples to prove it. Indeed, it was standard practice—tradition—for a warrior to compose and recite a poem as he lay dying.

It is important to remember that Tsurayuki is describing *Yamato-uta*, *Japanese* poetry, in particular. In that age, discussion of "poetry" usually implied works written in Chinese. The *Kokinshū*, Tsurayuki declares, anthologizes Japanese poetry instead.

The Significance of Imperial *Waka* Anthologies

Now, the *Kokinshū* was the first of what are known today as the *chokusen wakashū*, "imperial *waka* anthologies." The actual work of selecting and compiling the poems in the *Kokinshū* was left to Ki no Tsurayuki and a few others, but it was all done on the orders of Emperor Daigo. This national project was completed in the year 905, about a century before Murasaki Shikibu wrote the *Tale of Genji*.

The list of imperial *waka* anthologies eventually grew quite long. In the eleventh century, Emperor Shirakawa had Fujiwara no Michitoshi compile the *Goshūi wakashū* or "Later Gleanings" collection. In the twelfth century, the retired Emperor Go-Shirakawa commissioned a group of poets led by Fujiwara no Shunzei to create the *Senzai wakashū* or "Thousand Years" anthology. Fujiwara no Teika presented the *Shin Kokin Wakashū* or "New Kokin wakashū" to the court in 1205, almost three centuries after the original *Kokinshū*.

There had, of course, been other anthologies of poetry compiled by imperial order. The emperor played an important role in the cultural domain. In the century before the *Kokinshū*, Emperor Saga and Emperor Junna commissioned the compilation of three anthologies, including the *Keikokushū* or "National Polity Collection." But these contained Chinese poetry, not Japanese. And there were many other imperial collections of Chinese poetry before that.

Since the Nara period in the eighth century, if not before, Chinese had been the written language of governance in Japan. Regulations and legal codes were all in Chinese, as were official documents and correspondence. Literacy in the language was required for all of Japan's administrators and officials. I suspect that this had been the case since the age of Himiko, an ancient Japanese shaman queen who died around the middle of the third century, or possibly even earlier. National Treasure number 1 in Japan is the golden seal in Fukuoka City Museum that, as every Japanese schoolchild learns, reads "King of Na of Wa of Han" in Chinese. "Han" here refers to the Eastern Han dynasty in China, most likely dating this seal to the first century of the Common Era. "Wa" was the contemporary Chinese name for Japan, and "Na" was a kingdom within Japan at the time. The

King of Na received this seal from the reigning Han Emperor.

In this period, Chinese civilization was the center of East Asia. Japan and China must have had diplomatic relations of some sort already; the King of Na could hardly have received a seal like this without at least exchanging correspondence. Similarly, if there were relations between Himiko and Cao Wei, as described in the Chinese historical text *Records of the Three Kingdoms* (*San guo zhi),* they must have been conducted via documents written in Chinese. Writing is often said to have entered Japan in the fifth or sixth century, but the real date must have been considerably earlier, or establishing these sorts of relations with China would have been impossible.

In any case, in ancient Japan, Chinese literacy was essential. All officials could read and write the language, and of course students and ambassadors sent to China used it while they were there. In the Heian period, the scholar and statesman Sugawara no Michizane wrote marvelous poetry in Chinese. And, as I mentioned earlier, there were several imperial anthologies collecting Chinese lyrics by Japanese poets.

At the same time, people were writing poems in Japanese too—even Michizane. Awareness of the tradition of *Yamato-uta*, as opposed to Chinese poetry, gradually rose, and the *Kokinshū* was compiled as a sort of declaration of Japanese aesthetics. All this is in Tsurayuki's *kana* preface, which has *Yamato-uta*, "Japanese poetry," as its opening words.

Waka actually date back to far more ancient times. According to the early eighth-century *Record of Ancient Things* (*Kojiki*), the first *waka* was recited by the deity Susanoo no Mikoto:

yakumo tatsu	the eightfold fence of Izumo
Izumo yaegaki	where eightfold clouds rise:
tsumagomi ni	to enclose my wife
yaegaki tsukuru	I shall build an eightfold fence
sono yaegaki o	that eightfold fence!

Susanoo no Mikoto was probably legendary, but the earliest surviving *waka* were written in the age of the *Man'yōshū* anthology, centuries before the *Kokinshū*.

Shizuoka Prefecture recently compiled an anthology called *Mount Fuji: One Hundred Poems from One Hundred Poets* (*Fuji-san hyakunin isshu*) that I found to be excellent reading. It includes poems about Mount Fuji from poets ranging from Tawara Machi, who is still writing today, all the way back to ancient figures like Yamabe no Akahito and Kakinomoto no Hitomaro, active in the eighth and seventh centuries respectively. What's more, these poems from more than a millennium ago can still be understood by elementary school children today. Take Akahito's famous *waka* about Mount Fuji:

Tago no Ura yu	looking back as we leave
uchi-idete mireba	the Bay of Tago
mashiro ni zo	white indeed
Fuji no takane ni	on Fuji's peak
yuki wa furitsutsu	falls the snow

This represents a linguistic tradition that has survived all the way to modern times.

In France, in England, in Germany, people cannot understand the language their ancestors spoke in the eighth century. There are many magnificent old poems in these languages, but they don't start appearing until the late medieval or Renaissance periods. Before that, the Greek and Latin literary traditions were dominant across Europe. Those traditions had marvelous poetry of their own, of course, but they did not survive into modern times. Today's Europeans do not understand Latin, and use it only in special circumstances.

The earliest English poetry that a speaker of today's language might understand dates from the fourteenth or fifteenth century. Dante's fourteenth-century *Divine Comedy* is renowned for having been written in the Tuscan dialect, which is essentially modern Italian—although Dante also wrote poems in Latin, which was more usual at the time. In any case, it was only around the fourteenth century that poems in *vernacular* languages begin to appear in Europe.

Akahito's poem is centuries older, but its language remains comprehensible today. Histories of European literature cite works in languages like Middle English and Middle French, but these are no longer accessible to today's readers, except for scholars with special training—and unlike the carefully edited *Kokinshū*, these poems were preserved haphazardly at best. In Japan, however, the same linguistic tradition has continued since at least the *Kojiki*. This is something with few parallels anywhere in the world. I do not mean to imply that the Japanese themselves are superior in some way. There is simply nothing to compare the tradition of *Yamato-uta* to. It is a rare thing even in global terms.

The *Kokinshū* was the first to collect these poems in a systematic way, and its organizational structure was unique. There have been anthologies in the West since ancient times, too, but as a basic rule they are organized by author. For example, people of my generation often used an English collection called the *Golden Treasury* as a text in school. It has a section for Wordsworth, another for Byron, a third for Tennyson… but Japanese anthologies like the *Kokinshū* and *Man'yōshū* are not organized in this way.

The first sections of the *Kokinshū* are seasonal: a spring section, a summer section, and so on. The very first poem in the *Kokinshū* begins, "Before the year / is out, spring has come" (*toshi no uchi ni / haru wa kinikeri*). This is a poem of the New Year, the dawn of spring. After the poems of spring come the poems of summer, and the seasons continue until the year is out. Next come poems of celebration, poems of love, poems of travel, and other categories. Finally there are miscellaneous poems, and these too are subdivided by content.

As a result, the same author might appear in many places. If someone wants to read all the poems by Ki no Tsurayuki in an English collection, they can just turn to his section, but in the *Kokinshū* his works are scattered throughout the entire anthology. Thus, even the structure of the *Kokinshū* is unlike what is seen in the West. Nature is a particularly important organizational principle, and the same is true of all the imperial collections that followed, whose editors generally showed more interest in the natural world than authorial intent.

Consider one of the poems of celebration by Tsurayuki himself:

haru kureba	when spring comes
yado ni mazu saku	the first to flower in my yard

ume no hana	are the blossoms of the plum
kimi ga chitose no	which seem to me a garland
kazashi to zo miru	for your thousand years, my lord

According to the explanatory text, this was "written on the folding screen behind Prince Motoyasu at his seventieth birthday celebration." In Japan today, the sixtieth birthday is celebrated as *kanreki*, the completion of a full Chinese calendrical cycle. It seems that in the Heian period similar celebrations were held every ten years beginning at the age of forty, or indeed in honor of any particularly auspicious event. Poetry was recited at those celebrations, and many of these works are collected in the *Kokinshū*.

Now, recall that the explanatory text says "written on the folding screen behind Prince Motoyasu." A poem was recited and then written on the folding screen while the party was still going on. This makes that poem a *byōbu-uta*, "folding screen poem," a common genre back then, generously represented in the *Kokinshū* and other *waka* collections. The screen, on the other hand, was called an *uta-byōbu* or "poem folding screen." Unfortunately, none of the actual screens survive, but we know that people would compose a poem based on the painting and then add it to the screen as well, writing it either on the image directly or on a separate piece of paper that was then pasted on. In either case, uniting word and image opened up a rich, symphonic world, and this practice shows an exceptionally close link between poetry and painting in Japan since ancient times.

Crossing the Word—Image Border

Figure 1 is a National Treasure dating from the late Heian period known as the *Fan-shaped Album of the Lotus Sutra*. This is just one of many examples. As you can see, the words of the Lotus Sutra are written right over the picture on the fan. It would be difficult to find an example of this in another country. Outside Japan, people have always tended to write around pictures rather than over them. It makes the text easier to read. But as you can see from figure 1, the text on this fan is written over the picture. Nor does there seem to be any connection between word and image here. Experts have tried in vain to uncover one, but it seems to be just a genre painting with the words of a sutra written over it—a decorative picture plus text, uniting word and image.

Consider, also, the *Jeweled Stupa Mandala in Gold Script* (fig. 2), a work from the Kamakura period. In Buddhism, a stupa is an important structure for storing the relics of a Buddha; the stupa in this picture is at the center of the mandala, executed splendidly in gold on navy blue paper. Looking closely we can see that, on the ground floor, there is a Buddha inside—and that the roofs and walls are actually Chinese characters. In fact, every part of the building, right down to the bells hanging from the eaves, is text from the Lotus Sutra. This picture of an important stupa is a *moji-e*.

Figure 1. *Fan-shaped Album of the Lotus Sutra* (*Senmen Hokkekyō sasshi*), twelfth century. Shitennōji Temple. (See plate 1)

Figure 2. *Jeweled Stupa Mandala in Gold Script* (*Konji hōtō mandara*) (detail), twelfth to thirteenth century. Myōhōji Temple. Image: Sakai City Museum. (See plate 2)

Sori: A Plastic Sensitivity

Another notable feature of the *Jeweled Stupa Mandala* is the fact that the edges of the eaves curve very slightly upwards. This is actually a feature of all Japanese stupas and pagodas. The pagodas at Daigoji and Hōryūji are good examples of this design (fig. 3). This kind of curve, called *sori* in Japanese, is not often seen in other countries.

There are pagodas in China, too, and of course in India. In fact, the five-storied pagoda originates in India. The pagoda in figure 4 is a seven-storied one built by the Khitan people in the eleventh century. But notice that—and this may be partly due to local climate conditions—its eaves aren't very deep. The eaves on Chinese buildings usually protrude a fair distance, and some have a strong curl that goes almost all the way around—what you might call a curve taken to extremes. But in Japan, the curve is only slight. Figure 5 shows the Golden Hall at Tōshōdaiji Temple; all of the temples in Nara look like this.

In Japanese architecture, the roof is very important. Roofs are large and eaves are deep; they are the first part of a building that a visitor sees. The line of the traditional Japanese roof extends out horizontally, then curves up slightly at each end. Figure 6 shows the Reliquary Hall (*Shariden*) at Engakuji Temple in Kamakura, revealing that the same design was

Figure 3. Five-storied pagoda, Daigoji Temple.

Figure 4. Seven-storied pagoda, Khitan.

Figure 5. Golden Hall, Tōshōdaiji Temple.

Figure 6. Reliquary Hall (*Shariden*), Engakuji Temple.

used even in the Buddhist architecture of the Kamakura Period. Whether tiled or thatched with silvergrass or straw, roofs all had the same horizontal line with slightly curved ends. In the case of Engakuji, note also that it is surrounded by trees, placing it within nature.

The same forms are used in military architecture. Visitors from other countries are always interested in Japan's castles as well as its temples. Figure 7 shows Himeji Castle. This is military architecture—a fortress, in other words. And, as can be seen, its eaves curve slightly upwards at the edges, even though this serves no military purpose. But it is extremely beautiful and elegant—one can see why Himeji Castle was also known as "White Crane Castle."

The roof is the most important part of Japanese architecture, but we see the same curve on stone walls, too. In the early seventeenth century, the daimyo Katō Kiyomasa added curved stone walls to Kumamoto Castle, called "warrior-returners" (*musa-gaeshi*) because they were difficult to climb. The same idea was used at Edo Castle, where the stone walls had a similar *sori*.

As another kind of example, figure 8 is a picture of the sixth- and seventh-century statesman and scholar Prince Shōtoku. It is usually called the "Prince Asa" portrait, after the person said to have painted it in the late seventh or early eighth century. Note that Prince Shōtoku is wearing a belt with a buckle. There were no buckles or buttons on Japanese clothing originally. Something like the modern button was in use in Europe as early as ancient Greece, and was eventually followed by buckles. Japanese garments, however, use tied cords for this purpose. Even today, traditional

Figure 7. Himeji Castle.
(See plate 3)

Figure 8. *Portrait of Prince Shōtoku and Two Princes* (*Shōtoku Taishi oyobi ni ōji zō*), eighth century. Imperial Household Agency.

Japanese clothing is made entirely from textiles—and yet, in this picture Prince Shōtoku is using a buckle, introduced from China. Prince Shōtoku was a serious scholar who imported sutras to Japan and wrote commentaries on them, but we can see here that he also had a general interest in whatever was new, with a remarkably cosmopolitan fashion sense.

Now, look at the swords Prince Shōtoku is carrying. They are straight, like all the most ancient Japanese swords were. The iron sword from the Inariyama burial mound sword is straight, as is the seven-branched sword from Baekje in ancient Korea. But the sword carried by the figure to Shōtoku's left is slightly curved. The curve in Japanese swords appears once we enter the Heian period. It becomes their distinctive feature, and, again, it is the same *sori* that is found in roofs and castle walls.

European Curves, Japanese *Sori*

Sori is actually very difficult to translate into English. I have used "curve" above, but this word, along with its equivalents in other European languages, is defined in opposition to straight lines. The two are separate: straight lines on one hand, and curves on the other.

In Western architecture, curves have been used since ancient Roman times. Gothic and Renaissance buildings all use domes, cupolas, arches, and so on. These are all curved, and can be drawn with a compass or similar tool. For straight lines, however, a ruler is used: the two types of line are completely separate.

In Japan, carpenters use a taut length of cord to straighten the eaves in a new building, or to cut straight boards. When I was a child—and perhaps even today—carpenters carried something called a *sumitsubo*, literally "ink pot." This is similar to a Western chalk line, but uses ink instead. It contains a cord which is inked and pulled taut along the surface to be marked, then plucked so that it snaps against that surface and inks a straight line on it. Carpenters would follow that line to cut the board. Pulling the string taut left a straight line. Giving it a hint of slack would let the line sag. And note that the line of the eaves in traditional Japanese architecture matches that sag. In other words, *sori* is just a straight line with added slack; the two kinds of line are fundamentally the same thing. Descriptions of houses built according to traditional methods often include deductions like "The cord must have been stretched from here to here and then loosened slightly."

This is why simply translating *sori* as "curve" is misleading. From the Japanese perspective, *sori* is just a slightly altered straight line. In fact, in earlier times, carpenters specializing in shrines and palaces would also measure using a tool called a *tawami shaku*. A *shaku* is a unit of measure roughly equivalent to the foot, and *tawami shaku* literally means "slack *shaku*." A slack *shaku* was usually a long, thin board of Japanese cypress. Placed on a surface, it would lay flat; lifted at both ends, it would sag in the middle under its own weight. Carpenters are said to have shared secret traditions about this sag, including how to make the middle of the board slightly thicker to compensate for it.

If a slack *shaku* is held with one end much higher than the other, the sag in the middle shifts downward so that the overall shape is the same diagonal line ending in *sori* seen on the "warrior-returning" walls of Kumamoto Castle. Here, too, we find that a straight line and *sori* are fundamentally one. The same cord or measuring stick is used to make both. And this unity between the straight and the curved can also be found in Japan's writing system and poetic tradition.

The Plasticity of Hiragana

The calligraphy in figure 9 is the famous first poem of the *Kokin wakashū,* by Ariwara no Motokata:

toshi no uchi ni	before the year
haru wa kinikeri	is out, spring has come—
hitotose o	a single year, but
kozo to ya iwan	should it be called last year?
kotoshi to ya iwan	should it be called this year?

The poem is written entirely in hiragana, one of Japan's phonetic scripts. As the magnified figure alongside it shows, in the two-character sequence *hito* ひと from *hitotose* ("single year"), the last stroke of the *hi* ひ is also the first stroke of the *to* と. The two characters are not separate, but neither do they merge completely. As a rule, Chinese characters are written one by

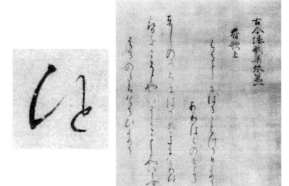

Figure 9. Ki no Tsurayuki (attributed), Kōya fragments of *Kokin wakashū* (*Kokin wakashū Kōyagire*), Vol. 1: "Spring, First Part," eleventh century. Gotoh Museum. (Left image: close-up of characters for *hito*.)

Figure 10. Ono no Komachi card from *Hyakunin isshu,* ca. 1660–1670. Yōmei Bunko Collection.

one as individual entities. But hiragana are so connected that a single stroke can span two characters.

In Japanese poetry, there is a technique called *kakekotoba*, usually translated "pivot words." As an example, consider these two lines:

konu hito o	waiting for someone who has not come
Matsuho no Ura no …	Matsuho Bay …

The underlined part is both the end of the sentence *Konu hito o <u>matsu</u>* ("<u>Waiting</u> for someone who has not come") and the start of the place name *<u>Matsu</u>ho no Ura* ("<u>Matsu</u>ho Bay"). Japanese poets have used the "pivot word" technique since ancient times; perhaps we could speak of "pivot characters" too.

It isn't clear exactly when kana came into use, but it was most likely the seventh or eighth century. By the time of the *Kokin wakashū*, kana were fully developed. Figure 10 is another stunning example of hiragana in use. This is a *karuta* card from the Yōmei Bunko collection with some lines from *One Hundred Poems from One Hundred Poets* (*Hyakunin isshu*) on it. We will come back to these cards, but note that the whole thing is written in hiragana, albeit very hard-to-read ones. This is actually the second half of Ono no Komachi's "Color of the flowers" poem, which we will return to as well.

In terms of historical development, the straight lines that came from Chinese characters mysteriously became curved in hiragana, inviting comparisons to the sensibility at work in the *sori* of a roof.

Comparing Japanese and Western Architecture

Let us turn to the world of architecture. Figure 11 shows the Parthenon, part of a UNESCO World Heritage Site in Greece and often compared to the Ise Grand Shrine in Japan (fig. 12). As you can see, it has two rows of columns with beams laid crosswise between them and a triangular roof on top. This is known as post-and-lintel construction. Supporting the roof is the most important task in architecture, and there are two ways to do it. The first is to use posts—columns or pillars. This is the traditional ap-

Figure 11. The Parthenon.　　　　Figure 12. The Ise Grand Shrine.

proach in Japan, as it is in most places where buildings tend to be made of wood, because trees are so easy to make into posts.

In Mesopotamia, on the other hand, buildings were made of brick. Bricks weren't suitable for building posts, so the Mesopotamians would stack them up and put an arch on top. The stone that served as a building material in Europe could be used either way, but was usually made into walls in the same way. As a result, since Roman times, Western architecture has been an architecture of walls. Gothic and other styles used columns in various ways, of course, but the walls were the most important element.

When arriving at a Japanese temple like Tōshōdaiji or Engakuji, the first thing that comes into view is the roof. On Western buildings like the Parthenon, it is the columns or walls that catch the eye; the roof is almost invisible. When Commodore Matthew Perry arrived at Japan in the nineteenth century and surveyed the city of Edo from his ship, he is said to have remarked that it was "nothing but roofs." It is true that, viewed from Edo Bay at that time, the city's roofs would have been very noticeable (see figure 13 for a similar view).

Because roofs are what make Japanese architecture unique, styles of architecture are actually distinguished by their roof design: gabled roofs, hipped gabled roofs, and so on. This contrasts with the West, where styles are defined by their period: Romanesque, Gothic, and the like.

Perry arrived in Japan in 1853. In 1860, as a return gesture, the shogunate dispatched an embassy to the United States. The embassy personnel traveled on a US naval vessel, but the Japanese *Kanrin Maru*, captained by Katsu Kaishū, made a point of accompanying them to prove that a Japanese vessel could make the voyage too. In fact, the *Kanrin Maru* was the first ship with an all-Japanese crew ever to cross the Pacific Ocean.

When the Japanese embassy arrived in San Francisco after a stopover in Hawaiʻi, their first impression is said to have been "American cities are nothing but walls." The walls were what caught their eye; that was the difference they noticed.

The Parthenon is a temple. This is the reason that it was made out of stone instead of timber, which was originally the norm for Greek dwellings, although none of those houses survive today. Each column of the Parthenon is actually made of smaller segments stacked on top of each other rather than carved out of a single stone. Note how shallow the eaves are, too. They do little more than cover the enclosed space.

As I mentioned, the Parthenon is often compared to the Ise Grand Shrine (fig. 12), which also uses posts and lintels. At the center is one of the *munamochibashira*, or "ridge-bearing pillars." This pillar supports one end of the ridge, and the roof as a whole is secured with forked finials called *chigi*. One major difference from the Parthenon is the extreme depth of the eaves. Not only does this enclose more space under the eaves themselves, it also makes the roof more eye-catching. Local geography and climate are partly involved here, no doubt—high levels of rainfall, perhaps, or strong winds.

Another important difference: at the Parthenon, the temple itself is the sacred space. The same applies to Christian churches in the West. Our world, the secular world, lies outside the church; only the interior of the building is sacred. In Japan, however, both the structure itself and its natural surroundings are considered the realm of the divine. The Ise Grand

Figure 13. Keisai Eisen, "Looking at Mount Fuji from Nihonbashi, Edo" (Edo Nihonbashi yori Fuji o miru zu) from *Eisen's Famous Places in Edo* (*Eisen Edo meisho*), nineteenth century. National Diet Library.

Figure 14.
Isuzu Forest and
The Ise Grand Shrine.

Shrine, for example, is surrounded by Isuzu Forest (fig. 14), and the entire region is sacred. Having crossed the Isuzu River, one is in the domain of the kami.

What Is a Torii?

Next I'd like to share a photograph of Notre-Dame Cathedral in Paris (fig. 15). The cathedral is the realm of the Christian God, of course, but the plaza before it is simply a meeting place—an entirely secular world—and this has always been so. Still, set one foot inside the building, and you are in the world of the divine.

How are things different in Japan? Figure 16 is a painting called *Kasuga Mandala*, dating to the Kamakura period, around the same time as Notre-Dame. Many types of structures can be seen in the painting. These are important, but these buildings are not the only sacred spaces. In fact, the entire area is sacred. Even Mount Kasuga in the background is a deity. The whole scene is the domain of the kami; the buildings were erected for the people who come to worship there.

How is the divine world distinguished from the secular one in Japan, if not through architecture as in the West? The answer can be seen toward the bottom of figure 16: a gate-like structure shaped something like a capital II (*pi*). This is called a *torii*, and it separates the domain of the kami from its secular surroundings. Even today, every shrine across Japan has a torii before it. Stepping through the torii, we enter a sacred space, leaving the secular world outside behind. However, in physical terms, a torii does nothing at all to make this distinction. It has no doors, and can easily be sidestepped in any case.

In the past, when visitors from outside Japan asked me what a torii was, I would reply, "It's the gate at the entrance to the domain of the kami." But in other countries, a "gate" or "entrance" is something that *must* be passed through to enter what lies beyond. The three entrances of Notre-Dame Cathedral, for example, are open during the day, but no one is permitted inside at night. The doors close, and inside and outside are completely cut off from each other. But a torii can be passed through at any time, or simply sidestepped. My foreign interlocutors did not understand how such a structure could make any distinction at all. In truth, the distinction is not physical but entirely in the Japanese mind. As a result, specialists today recognize that *gate* alone does not convey the meaning of *torii* in English, and simply call these structures *torii* or *torii gates*.

Figure 15. Notre-Dame Cathedral.

Figure 16. *Kasuga Mandala* (*Kasuga mandara*), thirteenth century. Tokyo National Museum. (See plate 4)

Figure 17. Miyajima.

Thus, torii are connected to nature, and because mountains are deities in Japanese religious thought, they often stand *within* nature, too. Figure 17 shows the famous torii at Miyajima in Aki, Hiroshima Prefecture. It stands on the foreshore, so that when the tide comes in it is partly submerged. Everything inshore from this torii—the entire island—is considered sacred.

Closeness to Nature in Japanese Aesthetics

Japan and the West treat nature entirely differently. Figure 18 is a photograph of the famous Gardens of Versailles. These are laid out in the classical French Garden style, which became a template for Western gardens in general. The flowerbeds have lateral symmetry; the human touch is obvious, and even the yews in the middle are carefully pruned into cones. The fountain is visible in the middle of the photograph, although the water is not in motion in this shot. The effect is stunning, but entirely the result of imposing an artificial order on nature.

In a Japanese garden, the human touch is supposed to be absent. Gardeners do all kinds of work and maintenance, of course, but the result does not have this artificial look. Figure 19 shows the garden of the Daisen'in subtemple within Daitokuji Temple, just in front of the building where the head of Daisen'in resides. Within this very limited space, a vision of the deep mountains is evoked to superb effect.

The Gardens of Versailles are so large that just strolling through them is exhausting. The garden at Daisen'in is tiny, but whole mountains and valleys have been created inside it. It is a rock garden, and the white sand and gravel in the middle give the impression of a waterfall. The goal was to recreate a natural wilderness in the limited space available. Of course, this was done by human beings who found the right rocks and arranged them just so, but to intentionally create something that looks like a natural mountain valley is an example of Japanese aesthetics at work.

Figure 18. Gardens of Versailles.

Figure 19. Garden outside Hōjō residence, Daisen'in, Daitokuji Temple. (See plate 5) Photo © Mizuno Katsuhiko

Then there is the matter of fountains, which are a must for Western gardens, and increasingly Japanese parks too. Figure 20 shows the fountains at the Gardens of Versailles in action. In Switzerland, they are very proud of the Jet d'eau in Lake Geneva, which shoots water hundreds of meters straight up—although I understand that a fountain that goes even higher has since been installed elsewhere. Since the seventeenth century, the Gardens of Versailles have had a complex of fountains shooting water high and low and at various angles to create something like a ballet performed by the water.

So fountains are a necessity for a Western garden. In fact, though, they are quite unnatural. Water runs downhill, but fountains send it back the other way. They are an exercise of human power in defiance of nature. In Japan, water has been used in gardens since ancient times, but always in the form of waterfalls or streams or ponds—always in accordance with nature.

Figure 20. Fountains, Gardens of Versailles.

Figure 21. Phoenix Hall (*Hōōdō*, Byōdōin Temple, Uji).

Figure 22. Eiffel Tower.

Figure 23. Daimonji bonfire.

Figure 21 is the Phoenix Hall (*Hōōdō*) at Byōdōin Temple at Uji, Kyoto. I understand it has been renovated, restored to its older form, but it was originally designed to be viewed from across the pond, as if looking over the water at the Pure Land. The work required around the pond to keep it filled has reportedly been challenging for a very long time. This is how water is used in Japanese gardens. Fountains are a recent Western import.

We see a similar difference in the Western fondness for towering monuments. This is a matter of urban planning. Monuments like the Eiffel Tower (fig. 22) and the Arc de Triomphe are placed right in the middle of the city. They are made to catch the eye. This is not done in Japan. Looking through Hiroshige's *One Hundred Famous Views of Edo* (*Meisho Edo hyakkei*), it becomes apparent that Edo had almost nothing that could be called a monument.

Even now, it is all but impossible to find a Japanese postcard that shows a building alone. A postcard of Himeji Castle will also show the cherry blossoms to full effect. Kinkakuji Temple might be depicted in the snows of winter.

Or the seasons might be evoked by a particular festival. At the famous Daimonji Festival in Kyoto, characters and images are recreated on the mountainside in bonfires; figure 23 shows the character *dai* 大, "big." (The *monji* part of the festival's name means "character"; the whole name is therefore something like "Festival of the character *dai*.") This custom was originally a farewell to the ancestral spirits that came home for Bon, but now it is a more general summer festival. Observances connected to the natural world like this show up throughout Japanese history.

The Four Seasons in Japanese Painting

We see similar patterns in art. Figure 24 shows a pair of painted four-panel folding screens known as the *Birds in Autumn and Winter* screens. These were originally one long screen, but are currently separated into two, left and right. The right screen shows a landscape as summer turns into autumn, with fall foliage around the middle. The left screen begins in autumn and ends, on the far left, with a snow-covered plain. The artist depicted the change of seasons from autumn to winter—hence the current name for the screens. There was probably a companion set of screens with the change from spring to summer painted on them, making a pair of eight-panel screens showing the full seasonal cycle, but these other screens are lost now.

Thus, the same painting has autumn leaves on the right and winter snow on the left. The seasons overlap in a single work. When Westerners see this, they ask, "Well, which is it—autumn or winter?" In the West, since at least the Renaissance, paintings have been expected to depict a single moment in time. But in Japan, time passes within the frame of the picture.

Combining this with the work of everyday people results in something like the *Scenes of Farming in the Four Seasons*, a pair of six-panel screens painted in the nineteenth century by a member of the Kanō School (fig.25). Starting on the right, one can see the cherry blossoms of spring,

Figure 24. *Birds in Autumn and Winter* (*Shūtō kachō-zu*), sixteenth century. Suntory Museum of Art.

Figure 25. Kanō Seisen'in Osanobu, *Scenes of Farming in the Four Seasons* (*Shiki kōsaku-zu*), Edo period (ca. 1825). Suntory Museum of Art.

both in the foreground and up in the mountains in the background. Not far away are people working in the rice paddies, followed by the rice nursery. The left screen has a river with people bathing in it—a summer scene. In the final few panels, on the left, people are bringing in the harvest. This is where the human activity ends, and there is snow on the mountains in the distance. This is another pair of screens depicting the change of seasons from spring to winter, but it includes scenes of daily life as well. Figure 26 shows a close-up of the harvest scene on the left, which also has people rejoicing, children playing, and so on—all these everyday scenes, depicted together.

This representative tradition has existed since ancient times. Japan had a convenient format called the *emakimono* or "picture-scroll" which allowed scenery to go on and on without a break. Figure 27 is part of a fa-

Figure 26. Detail from figure 25.

mous National Treasure called *Landscapes of the Four Seasons*, in the possession of the Mōri family. Painted by Sesshū, the full scroll is very long and depicts the change in seasons from spring to winter.

Even after the Meiji period and into modern times, we see works of this sort. Figures 28 and 29 are four-season landscapes from Hishida Shunsō and Yokohama Taikan respectively. These are both picture scrolls, the first painted in 1910 and the second in 1947, and, as the viewer unrolls them, the scenery changes from spring to summer to autumn and then to winter, all inside a single picture.

Emoji, *Moji-e*, and Play

Next I'd like to talk about emoji. As an example that illustrates the Japanese fondness for seasonal detail, consider figure 30, a letter to a friend from haiku poet Yosa Buson.

Figure 27. Sesshū, *Landscapes of the Four Seasons* (*Shiki sansui-zu*), 1486. Mōri Museum. (See plate 6)

Top: Figure 28. Hishida Shunsō, *Landscape of the Four Seasons* (*Shiki sansui*) (detail), 1910. (See plate 7) National Museum of Modern Art, Tokyo.

Bottom: Figure 29. Yokoyama Taikan, *Landscapes of the Four Seasons* (*Shiji sansui*) (detail), 1947. Yokoyama Taikan Memorial Hall.

It seems that Buson was out one day when he was caught in the rain on his way home. This friend's house was nearby, so he sheltered from the rain there a while. When the downpour showed no sign of letting up, he borrowed an umbrella and went home. The next day, he sent the umbrella back by messenger, and this is the letter he included with it. "Thank you for your hospitality yesterday," it reads. "The tea you served as I sheltered from the rain was delicious. I waited for my chance to go home, but the rain kept getting"—and here Buson draws a picture of the rain. Presumably he means "kept getting stronger," but he expresses that with a picture. It looks like the sort of thing a child would draw. Buson ends by saying "Here is the umbrella I borrowed," except that instead of using the word for "umbrella," he draws a picture of one. In other words, Buson used an emoji.

Figure 31 is another letter from Buson, also to a friend and fellow haiku poet. This is an extremely valuable item that has been designated an

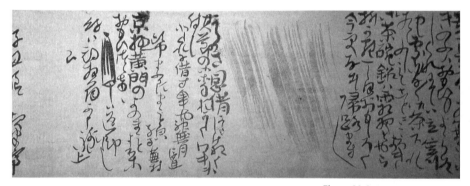

Figure 30. Letter from Yosa Buson, eighteenth century. Nomura Art Museum.

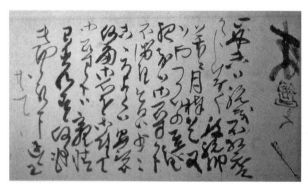

Figure 31. Letter to Tairaidō from Yosa Buson, eighteenth century. Agency for Cultural Affairs.

Important Cultural Property. The letter is addressed to "Tairaidō," the friend's pen name. The actual content is unremarkable, but the opening salutation (on the far right of the image) is intriguing. To write the name "Tairaidō," Buson begins with an oversized version of the character *rai* 来. This is a pun based on the fact that *tai*, the first element in his friend's name, literally means "big." A big *rai*, read "Tairai." After that is a small picture of a *dō*, a type of building in Buddhist architecture, so that the whole is read "Tairaidō." And then comes the part roughly corresponding to "Dear," in hiragana as usual.

Beneath this salutation, in the place where a Japanese letter-writer would usually write their own name, Buson has drawn a picture of an arrow with half of its fletching removed. In Japanese, "arrow" is *ya* and "half" is *han*, so this picture is read "Yahan." This is a reference to Buson's poet name, "Yahantei II"—the first Yahantei was his teacher. He is using the picture of the half-fletched arrow as a sort of signature. Haiku poets of this period often engaged in this sort of game, which constitutes a form of emoji.

This sort of thing was very popular among Edoites in general. Consider figure 32, an ukiyo-e by Katsushika Hokusai. This is a print, so many copies were made. Presumably it was quite a hit. It is from a series called *The Six Poetic Immortals*, and it depicts the poet known as Kisen Hōshi, "Kisen the Priest." The ornamented top half of the paper has one of Kisen's poems written on it:

wa ga io wa	my little hut
miyako no tatsumi	lies southeast of the capital
shika zo sumu	and so I dwell
yo o ujiyama to	amid the hills of Uji
hito wa iu nari	woeful, so they say

The calligraphy is written in a rather scattered fashion. It cannot be read simply by starting at the top. The text does start on the right, but each column gradually sinks lower until leaping up to the top for "and so I dwell." The same sort of leap occurs in the poem's second half. Serious thought was given to the design of this layout.

Outside Japan, poems are always written with the lines neatly aligned.

Veering back and forth like this poem is simply not done. But in Japan, if anything, this is the norm. The placement of characters is a design element.

Below the poem is a picture of Kisen himself of the sort that might appear on a set of *karuta*. Note that the lines of his robe are somewhat emphasized. This is, of course, intentional. In fact, it is a message to the reader that the picture should be "read," too: the robes spell out *Kisen Hōshi* in hiragana. Kisen himself is drawn as a *moji-e*. In this series, Ono no Komachi, Ōtomo no Kuronushi, and the other poetic immortals are drawn in the same way, with their clothing spelling out their names in kana. This is a kind of play in which pictures and words are made one.

Next, an example incorporating a poem by Kakinomoto no Hitomaro:

honobono to	dimly, faintly
akashi no ura no	off Akashi Bay
asagiri ni	in the mists
shimagakure-yuku	I think on the boat that slips
fune o shi zo omou	away behind the islands

Figure 32. Katsushika Hokusai, "Kisen Hōshi," from *The Six Poetic Immortals* (*Rokkasen-zu*), nineteenth century. Hiragana characters used to draw the image are shown in the image below, from the catalog for the 1996 exhibition *A Genealogy of Moji-e and Emoji* (*Moji-e to emoji no keifu*), held at the Shōtō Museum of Art.

Figure 33. Hakuin, *Portrait of Hitomaro* (*Hitomaro zō*), Edo period. Sano Museum.

This poem is so well known that it is even quoted in the introduction to the *Kokin wakashū*. Hitomaro, also known as the "Saint of Poetry," was popular right through to the Edo period, and this is his best-known poem of all. Figure 33 is a picture incorporating the poem drawn by Hakuin, an Edo-period Zen priest from Shizuoka. The *honobono to* is in the middle, the *fune* is the head, and so on. The picture is of Hitomaro himself, and the pose, with his knees raised, is the one he is usually drawn in.

Word and Image Together

Figure 34 is part of a very famous work of art from the Edo period: a hand-scroll with silver and gold background by Tawaraya Sōtatsu and calligraphy by Hon'ami Kōetsu. Due to the cranes in the background, it is generally called the *Crane Scroll*.

Here, Kōetsu has written Hitomaro's "Dimly, faintly" poem directly over Sōtatsu's original painting of the cranes. The cranes are silver and the ground beneath them is gold—a very luxurious combination. It would be unthinkable to write a poem over the original artwork in the West. In fact, no one in Japan today who had a painting by Sōtatsu would dream of writing on it either.

When poems were added to pictures in China, they were written in

Figure 34. Tawaraya Sōtatsu (painting), Hon'ami Kōetsu (calligraphy), *Crane Scroll* (*Tsuru shita-e wakakan*), seventeenth century. Kyoto National Museum. (See plate 8)

Figure 35. Tawaraya Sōtatsu (painting), Hon'ami Kōetsu (calligraphy), *Deer Scroll* (*Shika shita-e wakakan*), seventeenth century. Yamatane Museum of Art.

whatever space was available. The picture was completed first, and then a poem was added in some blank area. Here, however, Kōetsu casually writes the poem right across the picture, creating a kind of collaborative work.

Hitomaro's name is at the bottom right, and the rest of the text is the poem. It is partly written using *man'yōgana*—Chinese characters used for sound alone in a system that dates to the *Man'yōshū* anthology. Some of these *man'yōgana* survived the creation of hiragana, leading to variants called *hentaigana* ("variant kana") that remained in use until the Edo period.

In this picture, the first *ho* is written using the standard modern *hiragana* ほ, but the *no* after it is one of these *hentaigana*—a kana character based on the Chinese character 農. After this come two pairs of dots that serve as repeat marks, giving *honobono*. (The *h* becomes *b* for phonetic reasons.)

The poem continues line by line, although note that the *shi* of *shima* (island) is long and thin, echoing the legs of the cranes. The combined effect is superb.

The same is true of the detail from the *Deer Scroll* in figure 35. Here, too, Kōetsu has written the poem over Sōtatsu's painting, this time of a deer on pale, thinly drawn ground. This poem is by Saigyō, whose name is also at the bottom right.

kokoro naki	even the heartless
mi ni mo aware wa	would surely feel
shirarekeri	something
shigi tatsu sawa no	snipes taking flight
aki no yūgure	in an autumn marsh by evening

This one is harder to read. *Hentaigana* are used for part of the first line, and the first two hiragana characters, *koko* ここ, are little more than dots.

In fact, there is an old poem about those two pairs of dots, which were such a common way of writing *ko* that this kana character was known as *futatsu moji*, the "double character." I heard this poem often in my youth:

futatsu moji	double character
ushi no tsuno moji	ox's horn character
sugu na moji	straight character

> *magari moji to zo* crooked character
> *kimi o oboyuru* is how I think of you

The "double character" is *ko* こ as noted above. The ox's horn character is *i* い. The straight character is *shi* し and the crooked character is *ku* く. The whole spells out *koishiku*, meaning roughly "with longing," providing the answer to the poem.

In the *Deer Scroll*, too, *ko* is written as two dots, and there are two sets of two, so this is *koko-*. Then comes *-ro naki* in *man'yōgana*, and things proceed to the next line. Here, too, we find a long, straight *shi* し alongside the deer's tail, echoing the shape of its leg. The leg is by Sōtatsu, the *shi* by Kōetsu. Next comes *shigi tatsu sawa no*, and, finally, a little way off, *aki no yūgure*. The placement of the characters, the style of calligraphy, and the combination of Chinese characters, *man'yōgana*, and hiragana all add up to a wonderful design that merges perfectly with the picture.

Chirashigaki and Kaeshigaki

The next examples are from a group of documents known as *tsugi shikishi*, literally "patched colored paper," dating to the Heian period. Then as now, poems were usually written on colored paper. Figure 36 is actually two pieces of paper "patched" together horizontally, illustrating how these works got their name. Despite the large gap in the middle, this is not two poems but one. The vertical placement of the lines rises and falls, and the text is an anonymous love poem from the *Kokin wakashū*:

> *tsukubane no* Mount Tsukubane
> *kono mo kano omo ni* on this side and that
> *kage wa aredo* offers its shelter

—and then, after a diagonal gap—

> *kimi ga mikage ni* but your shelter
> *masu kage wa nashi* no other could surpass

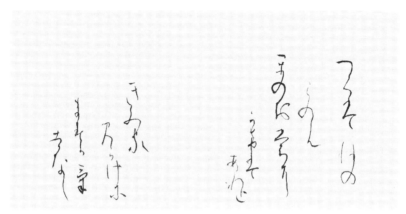

Figure 36. "Mount Tsukubane" calligraphy, *Tsugi Shikishi*. Fujita Art Museum.

The two parts are intentionally separated. This calligraphic technique exhibits an outstanding design sensibility and is known in Japanese as *chirashigaki*, "scattered writing." Calligraphy involving Japanese poetry is usually "scattered" to some extent.

The most extreme form of *chirashigaki* is known as *kaeshigaki*, "returned writing," in which not even right-to-left order is observed for the columns of text. Figure 37, a poem by Kiyohara no Fukayabu, is a representative example of this. The first part of the poem starts from the highest point, where the ink is darkest, and proceeds in columns to the left as usual:

hito o omou	a heart that longs
kokoro wa kari ni	for another is not
aranedomo	a wild goose, and yet
kumoi ni …	in the clouds …

At this point, the text skips to the far right for the conclusion:

… nomi mo	… alone
nakiwataru kana	does it call as it flies

In other words, the text as written is arranged something like this:

nomi mo naki
wataru
kana
hito o omou kokoro
wa kari ni aranedomo
kumoi ni

This clearly defies the convention of writing vertically from right to left, but more freedom was allowed for poetic calligraphy. Note also that the whole is arranged into a centered, triangular design.

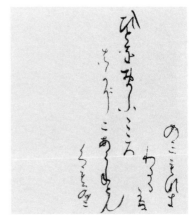

Figure 37. "A heart that longs" calligraphy. Tokyo National Museum.

The Uniqueness of Chinese Characters in Japan

Figure 38 is an interesting example I saw at a recent ukiyo-e exhibition. The poem is by Saigyō. Note that the Chinese characters 世間, "world," are positioned prominently in the middle. If read as Sino-Japanese vocabulary, this would be *seken*, but in this poem it is assigned the native Japanese reading *yo no naka*, with the same meaning. This is an example of something that I believe is unique to Japan: adopting Chinese characters while preserving its native language.

For example, when the Chinese characters 山 "mountain" and 川 "river" were adopted in Japan, they were pronounced in an approximation of the Chinese of the time—*san* and *sen* respectively. But in Japan, the same characters can also be pronounced or "read" *yama* and *kawa*, representing the native Japanese words for "mountain" and "river" respectively. These different pronunciations, known respectively as *on* "phonetic" and *kun* "interpretive" readings, are still in use today, and most Chinese characters used in Japan have at least one of each type. For example, the *kokin waka* part of the title *Kokin wakashū* could also be pronounced *inishie-ima no yamato-uta*. Of course, this does make studying the characters a challenge, since both *on* and *kun* pronunciations must be memorized.

This is not seen anywhere else in the East Asian cultural sphere where

Figure 38. *Beauty Leaning on an Armrest* (*Kyōsoku ni motareru bijin*), Edo period.

Chinese characters were adopted, which includes countries like Vietnam, Korea, and Mongolia. As is well known, Korea later switched to Hangul, a sound-based writing system. There is some talk of going back to Chinese characters, but basically everything is in Hangul now. Vietnam has adopted the Roman alphabet.

But Japan has kept Chinese characters alongside its phonetic kana. Even today, the standard orthography combines the two. Kana are ultimately derived from Chinese characters, of course, but in such a drastically changed form that they have become something entirely different. In Chinese characters, straight lines are fundamental, particularly vertical ones. Calligraphers even have a saying, "first, join heaven and earth," and Chinese characters were originally used in rituals of divination. In any case, the characters we use today are suited to vertical writing. When it is necessary to write them horizontally, this makes the designer's task more difficult. Even business cards commonly use a Ming typeface, in which the vertical lines are slightly thicker than the horizontal ones. The fundamental emphasis is on verticality.

Chinese characters also tend to have vertical symmetry. This can be seen in a range of basic characters:

一	one	二	two	三	three		
大	large	中	medium center	小	small		
山	mountain	川	river	草	grass	木	tree
日	sun Sunday	月	moon Monday	火	fire Tuesday	水	water Wednesday
木	tree Thursday	金	metal Friday	土	earth Saturday		
東	east	西	west	南	south	北	north

Of course, there are many other, more complex, characters made by combining different elements, but the tendency in these basic characters is toward straight lines and vertical symmetry.

The Roman alphabet also tends towards straight lines, with occasional exceptions like O and P that use circular shapes—perfect circles or ellipses like domes or arches. There is also a tendency towards symmetry, although the line of symmetry is more often horizontal, matching the direction of writing. The letter A has vertical symmetry, but B, C, D, and E all have horizontal symmetry. H, I, M, or T, U, V, W, X, Y—all of these have horizontal or vertical symmetry, or even both. This makes them easier to grasp as symbols as well as to write.

But in the complete set of hiragana, mysteriously enough, there is not a single straight line or instance of symmetry. And these are the characters that came into common use in Japan.

Figure 38 shows a painting with a poem written above it. The poem is from *Poems of a Mountain Home* (*Sankashū*) by Saigyō, a Buddhist priest of the Heian period. There is a story behind it. Saigyō was on his way home from visiting a temple when night began to fall. He came to a village

88

called Eguchi, and because the sun was going down and the weather was bad, he asked at one of the houses whether they would let him stay the night. The lady of the house, however, turned him down. The poem is Saigyō's lament at her cruelty in refusing him even a single night's shelter.

yo no naka o	to despise
itou made koso	this world of ours
katakarame	is hard indeed—
kari no yadori o	even fleeting shelter
oshimu kimi kana	you begrudge me

The word *kari* means both "borrowed" and "fleeting." The most prominent characters are 世間 in the middle of the page, here read *yo no naka* as noted above. The text then continues to the right column by column until leaping back to just left of the first column for the final *kimi kana*.

To the left of this is the woman's reply:

yo o itou	as you despise
hito to shi kikeba	our world, or so I hear
kari no yado ni	on fleeting shelter
kokoro tomu na to	you should not set your heart
omou bakari zo	it seems to me

The lines of the woman's reply are read downwards and to the left as usual. This combines with Saigyō's poem to create a sort of mountain-shaped arrangement of text. The picture of the woman below is artfully composed so that she is all but triangular as well.

This poem by Saigyō was very well known. It was used in ukiyo-e, Noh plays, and so on, ensuring that it would spread among not just the literati but the common folk, too. Regarding the woman Saigyō spoke to, the anthologies of his work record only that her name was "Tae," but it is important to note that the story is set in Eguchi, a harbor town with its own pleasure quarters. The woman was a courtesan. There were various elaborations on this story, one of the best known of which involves the woman actually being an incarnation of Kannon, Bodhisattva of compassion. This is also the plot of the Noh play *Eguchi*. In any case, the woman depicted in this painting is in fact a courtesan.

Word and Image in Handcraft Design

As an example from a different medium, consider figure 39. This is the lid of the "Hatsune" *Maki-e* Box, made for the daughter of Iemitsu, third Tokugawa shogun, on the occasion of her marriage. As befits a shogun's daughter, her trousseau was full of highly luxurious items. Many of these are still in the possession of the Tokugawa Art Museum, including a chest of drawers, a kimono rack, cosmetic paraphernalia, and of course this box. The "Hatsune" in the box's name reveals its intimate connection to literature: it refers to the ornamentation on the lid, which depicts a scene from a chapter in the *Tale of Genji* known as "Hatsune".

Hatsune is the name of a ceremony held early in the New Year. It involved children uprooting small pine trees, whose long, trailing roots were considered an auspicious symbol of longevity. Also known as *nebiki* or "root-pulling," this observance was formally called *hatsune* because it took place on the first (*hatsu*) day of the mouse (*ne*) after the New Year. Because this was also the start of spring, when warblers started to make themselves

Figure 39. "Hatsune" *Maki-e* Box (*Hatsune maki-e tebako*), seventeenth century. Tokyo National Museum. Image: TNM Image Archives. Hiragana characters used to draw the image are shown in the image below, from the catalog for the 1996 exhibition *A Genealogy of* Moji-e *and* Emoji (*Moji-e to emoji no keifu*), held at the Shōtō Museum of Art. (See plate 9)

heard, the name was also interpreted as meaning "first (*hatsu*) song (*ne*)."

In the "Hatsune" chapter of the *Tale of Genji*, Genji becomes intimate with a woman he meets during his exile on Akashi. Known only as the "Lady of Akashi," she gives birth to his child, but before long he must return to the capital. He takes the child with him, and calls for Akashi later. However, her social standing is too low to live with them. Concerned about her child, the Lady of Akashi sends Genji an assortment of correspondence at New Year's that includes a poem:

toshitsuki o	let she who has waited
matsu ni hikarete	months and years, drawn
furu hito ni	always to the pine
kyō uguisu no	hear this day the warbler's
hatsune kikaseyo	first spring song

"Months and years": Akashi herself is getting older. "Drawn always to the pine": in the original, *matsu* is actually a pivot word; it appears in the translation above as both "waited" and "pine." Akashi's wait to see her daughter has been long. Her request to hear "the warbler's first spring song" is actually a plea for some word from her daughter. And so Genji has her daughter write a reply in her childish way. The design on the box encapsulates this entire story.

Looking closely, we can see a splendid mansion on the left. On the roof and scattered elsewhere about are *aoi* (wild ginger) crests; these are used liberally in the design, as this was the crest of the Tokugawa family. On the right is a large pine tree. The top of the tree is rather oddly shaped, and this is because it is actually the *hentaigana* for *to*, based on the Chinese character 登. Similarly, the trunk of the tree is an extended *shi* し, and below that is the Chinese character 月, here read *tsuki*. This gives us most of the poem's first line already. The word *matsu* ("waited/pine") does not appear, but this is a picture of a pine, so the *matsu ni* is taken as given. The kana characters for *hikarete* are hidden elsewhere in the picture, scattered above in a form known as *ashide* or "reed hand."

By now we have the first two lines of the poem, and since everybody knew the *Tale of Genji* well in those days, that would have been enough: "Ah, this is the Lady of Akashi's poem from 'Hatsune.'" The ability to recognize references like this—and they were not rare—was a sign of cultural literacy.

One more. Figure 40 is a writing box ornamented with a poem by Fujiwara no Shunzei. Here the text stands out very clearly. The poem is about cherry-blossom viewing, and only the first half is on the lid:

> *mata ya mimu*   will I see its like again?
> *Katano no mino no*   cherry blossom viewing
> *sakuragari*   on the fields of Katano

—although the last line, *sakuragari* ("cherry blossom viewing") is represented by the content of the painting rather than in characters. Removing the lid, we find the rest of the poem inside the box:

> *hana no yuki furu*   a snow of flowers falls
> *haru no akebono*   early dawn in spring

These characters, too, are integrated into the picture. The ornamentation unites word and image into a stunning whole.

As a final example, consider the Pontoon Bridge *Maki-e* Writing Box by Hon'ami Kōetsu (fig. 41). A pontoon bridge is a provisional solution for crossing a river when no permanent bridge is available, made by lining up

Figure 40. Ogata Kōrin (design), Cherry Blossom Viewing *Maki-e* and Mother-of-Pearl Writing Box (Sakuragari maki-e raden kanagai suzuribako), Edo period. Fujita Art Museum. (Left: interior of box; right: lid.)

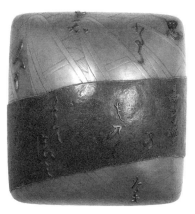
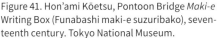

Figure 41. Hon'ami Kōetsu, Pontoon Bridge *Maki-e* Writing Box (Funabashi maki-e suzuribako), seventeenth century. Tokyo National Museum.

boats across the water and laying planks on top of them. The lid of this writing box actually depicts a pontoon bridge like this. The startling bulge at the center is an example of Kōetsu's bold design sensibility.

The piece is executed in *maki-e*, and there are boats drawn on the gold part. A plate of lead on top of these represents the boards of the bridge, and, of course, it has text on it. The *chirashigaki* makes it hard to read, but it is a poem by Minamoto no Hitoshi:

azumaji no	like the pontoon bridge
Sano no funahashi	of Sano in the east
kakete nomi	my longing spans
omoiwataru o	the space between us
shiru hito zo naki	though no one knows

Looking at the lid from above, *azumaji no* is written in gold on the right-hand end of the lead "bridge." The center of the bridge has *Sano no*. The word *funahashi* is not actually written; the pontoon bridge design itself serves as a kind of emoji representing it. *Kakete nomi* is at the left-hand end of the bridge. We leap up to the top right for *omoi-*, and then left for *-wataru*. Then back up for *o shiru hito zo*, and, finally, *naki* is below the bridge. The poem is completely scrambled; no one who did not know it already would be able to read it. This is a highly impressive work.

Fujiwara no Teika's Aesthetics of Rejection

Hundreds of years after Minamoto no Hitoshi, in the early thirteenth century, we arrive at the age of the *Shin kokin wakashū*, literally the "New *Kokin wakashū*." This is one of the most famous poems in the anthology, by Fujiwara no Teika:

koma tomete	to stop their horse
sode uchiharau	and brush off their sleeves
kage mo nashi	there is not a soul
Sano no watari no	at the Sano ford
yuki no yūgure	on a snowy evening

Once more we are at the crossing at Sano in the east. The snow is falling, and all is deserted and still. The first two lines suggest a human figure—in fact, "brush off their sleeves" implies a nobleman. But then Teika informs us that there was "not a soul" around to do any such thing.

How might this be depicted in a painting? Since nobody is around, it would just be an empty, snowy landscape. But rather than saying this directly, Teika first evokes the image of a noble on a horse brushing the dust of the road off his sleeves before rejecting this: there is no such person.

Figure 42. Ogata Kōrin, Sano Ford *Maki-e* Writing Box (*Sano no watari maki-e suzuribako*), Edo period (eighteenth century). Gotoh Museum.

This is a marvelous rhetorical approach. The *Kokinshū* was more straight-forward, but in the *Shin kokinshū*, Teika describes something splendid and then rejects it. I call this the "aesthetics of rejection," and the first few lines of another of Teika's poems are a typical example:

miwataseba	surveying the view,
hana mo momiji mo	of flowers and autumn leaves
nakarikeri …	there is no sign …

A stunning autumn tableau is evoked in the first two lines, only to be rejected in the third.

This recalls a *Kokinshū* poem by Sosei:

miwataseba	surveying the view,
yanagi sakura o	drooping willows mix
kokimazete	with cherry blossoms
miyako zo haru no	into a rich brocade
nishiki narikeru	of spring in the capital

Teika, of course, knew this poem, and it was with its vivid imagery in mind that he wrote the first two lines of his own poem, which summon up a similarly striking image—only to reject it in line three. There is nothing like that, he says, only:

… ura no tomaya no	… a rush-thatched hut
aki no yūgure	by the bay in autumn dusk

A solitary hut thatched with rushes, and nothing more: such are Teika's aesthetics.

Considering again how one might depict this technique visually, in this case we can find one answer in the Sano Ford *Maki-e* Writing Box by Ogata Kōrin, currently in the collection of the Gotoh Museum (fig. 42). On its lid is drawn the dazzling figure of a nobleman stopping his horse and brushing off his sleeves. This is exactly what the poem rejects, but the result is that people remember the poem itself. The design sparks a chain of associations leading all the way to "Ah, that lonely evening at Sano." This is a highly refined approach to aesthetic expression.

Designing Ariwara no Narihira's "Eight Bridges"

The most famous work to emerge from the Rinpa School is surely the painting *Yatsuhashi* (fig. 43). The poem written on it is from the *Tales of Ise*:

karagoromo	familiar as
kitsutsu narenishi	a robe long worn
tsuma shi areba	is my wife, and so
harubaru kinuru	having come so far
tabi o shi zo omou	I brood on my journey

Taking the first mora from each line gives *ka-ki-tsu-ha-ta*, which by the orthographic rules of the time was equivalent to *kakitsubata*, "irises." This is a scene from the *Tales of Ise*, during the section in which Ariwara no Narihira travels east. He has left the capital and come as far as Mikawa province. Today this is the eastern part of Aichi Prefecture, where the place name "Yatsuhashi," meaning "eight bridges," is still in use. The name

Figure 45. Ogata Kōrin, *Irises at Yatsuhashi (Eight Bridges)* (*Yatsuhashi-zu byōbu*), ca. 1710. Metropolitan Museum of Art. (See plate 10)

Figure 43. Ogata Kenzan, *Yatsuhashi* (*Yatsuhashi-zu*), eighteenth century. Agency for Cultural Affairs.

Figure 44. Ogata Kōrin, Yatsuhashi *Maki-e* Box (Yatsuhashi no maki-e tebako), eighteenth century. Tokyo National Museum.

Figure 46. Ogata Kōrin, *Irises* (*Kakitsubata-zu byōbu*), eighteenth century. Nezu Museum.

reflects a time when there were indeed many bridges in the area, allowing passage across the many forks of the large river there. (In ancient Japan, "eight" was sometimes used to just mean "many" or "countless.") Narihira's party found irises blooming there, and he was asked to compose a poem on that theme. Thinking back on his home in the capital, this is what he came up with. The episode became very widely known.

The painting in figure 43 is by Ogata Kenzan and depicts the "eight bridges" and the irises with the text of the poem scattered around them. It is a stunning work, the perfect union of word and image. As it happens, Ogata Kōrin also created a work on the same theme, albeit with no text: the Yatsuhashi *Maki-e* Box (fig. 44), a National Treasure. The irises are done in mother-of-pearl, while the bridges are lead plate. And then there are the famous *Irises at Yatsuhashi (Eight Bridges)* screens (fig. 45), currently at the Metropolitan Museum of Art, where the bridges and the irises are once more visible.

Normally, Narihira and his companions would be depicted as well. But none of these works include anything of the sort: they limit themselves solely to the irises and the bridges. In the extreme case, even the bridges are left out, as in the *Irises* screen at the Nezu Museum (fig.46). This is also based on Narihira's poem, but people from outside Japan find this difficult to understand. "What makes this Yatsuhashi?" I am often asked. "Exactly where are these flowers supposed to be blooming?" Well—in the water, of course. In the West, any rivers or other bodies of water in the scene would naturally be included in the painting, along with the banks, the sky, and so on. But in this work, all of that is rejected, leaving a stunning image of irises alone that is also grounded in literature and poetry.

Ono no Komachi's "Color of the Flowers"

Now let us return to the *Hyakunin isshu* cards from the Yōmei Bunko collection I mentioned earlier. Figure 47 is the pair of cards for Ono no Komachi's poem:

hana no iro wa	the color of the flowers
utsurinikeri na	has faded and passed on
itazura ni	in vain

Figure 48. Ono no Komachi. Edo-period parody from *Edo Hyakunin isshu*, ca. 1731.

Figure 47. Ono no Komachi cards from *Hyakunin isshu*, ca. 1660–1670. Yōmei Bunko Collection.

wa ga mi yo ni furu	have I spent my life
nagame seshi ma ni	watching the long rains fall

The first card has a portrait of Komachi herself and the first two lines of the poem, because that is all that is read aloud in the game of *karuta*. The original *Ogura hyakunin isshu* was compiled by Fujiwara no Teika while he was living on Mount Ogura, Kyoto, and was very widely known from the Momoyama period onward. This *Kōrin hyakunin isshu* has paintings by Kōrin both on the card to be read aloud and the card to be claimed by the players—and very impressive paintings they are, too.

The work became so well known that parodies appeared. Figure 48 is an example from the Edo period. Under the title "Ono no Komachi," it reads:

hana no koro wa	cherry blossom season
sakarinikeri na	has reached its peak
Uenoyama	on Ueno Hill
wa ga mi bentō	have I opened
hiraki seshi ma ni	my *bentō* boxed lunch

Great crowds of people come to view the cherry blossoms and eat boxed lunches at Ueno Park even today.

The existence of this parody indicates how widely Komachi's poem was known—there would be no point in parodying it otherwise. In other

Figure 49. Aoki Shigeru, *Illustrated* Karuta *Cards* (*E-karuta*), 1904.

Figure 50. Kizu Fumiya, *Distant Thoughts* (*Tōki omoi*), 2003. Private Collection.

words, the tradition dating back to the *Kokin wakashū* was still alive and well in Edo times.

And, in fact, beyond. Figure 49 is a *karuta* card painted by Meiji artist Aoki Shigeru. This card has the first three lines of the poem, in a calligraphic hand I find quite stunning. Aoki created many sets of illustrated *karuta* like this.

Finally, with figure 50 we arrive at a contemporary artist: Kizu Fumiya, born in Shizuoka Prefecture and now a professor at Tokyo University of the Arts. Komachi's poem is partly obscured by the leaves, but remains perfectly identifiable. At a glance, this seems to be a poem written on a sheet of paper, which was then pasted on to another, with leaves overhanging the scene. In fact, though, the entire tableau is one painting—a very interesting example, I think, of Super-Realistic painting.

Thus we see that word and image have coexisted in Japanese aesthetics right up to the present day.

Word and Image Separated: Text Design in the West

In the West, as Michel Foucault observed, word and image have been completely separate domains since the Renaissance, strictly prevented from intersecting. In medieval bibles and chronicles, illustrators experimented with various approaches to designing cover illustrations and frontispieces. Figure 51 shows a rather ornamental frontispiece with the opening words of the Gospel of John in Latin: *In principio*, "In the beginning." The design even includes the four evangelists in the corners. But in the rest of the text, the ornamentation is kept separate from the words.

Figure 52 is from the "Moxon Tennyson," a very fine illustrated anthology of Alfred Tennyson's poetry published in the nineteenth century by Edward Moxon. This is the first page of "The Lady of Shalott"; the poetry itself is set in printed type, and above is an illustration by the Pre-Raphaelite painter William Holman Hunt. Poetry and illustration are separate domains; word and image are kept apart.

A few decades later, however, William Morris thought that they might

Figure 51. Examples of medieval Bible frontispiece (ninth century) and main text (seventh century).

Figure 53. William Morris, *The Works of Geoffrey Chaucer*, 1896. Wayō Women's University Media Center Library.

Figure 52. William Holman Hunt, "The Lady of Shalott" from *Poems by Alfred Tennyson*, 1862.

be brought a little closer together. An example from one of his "Kelmscott editions," named for a manor he rented in Oxfordshire, can be seen in figure 53. The ornamentation is certainly heavier than in the Moxon Tennyson, but it is still arranged *around* the text. Apart from the illuminated initial capital, text and ornament are entirely separate. There is no sign of word and image intersecting the way they did in Japan.

The first European example of such an intersection was a book called *Poems of the Dragonfly* (*Poèmes de la libellule*), a collection of Japanese poems translated into French and published in the 1880s. Figure 54 shows a poem by Semimaru:

kore ya kono	so this is it—
yuku mo kaeru mo	where those coming and going
wakarete wa	part ways, and
shiru mo shiranu mo	friend and stranger meet—
Ōsaka no seki	the Osaka Barrier

Semimaru and the Osaka Barrier are on the left of the two-page spread, and the Japanese original poem is written in *chirashigaki* there, too. The French translation is on the right, sharing the page with a swarm of dragonflies in flight. The text is rather small and scattered about, but the largest

Figure 54. *Poems of the Dragonfly* (*Poèmes de la libellule*) (frontispiece and interior spread), 1885.

typeface is used for the translation, the slightly smaller block of text for the romanized Japanese, and the name "Semimaru" is among the dragonflies.

This frontispiece of *Poems of the Dragonfly* is also interesting. It was actually painted by a Japanese artist, Yamamoto Hōsui, who was in Paris at the time. A dragonfly perches on the plate bearing the French title, and the Japanese title is written on its wings in Chinese characters: 蜻蛉集, *Seireishū*. Even the year is written in Japanese. In other words, it was the end of the nineteenth century before word and image were finally united in France—in a form directly inherited from Japan.

Among the readers amazed by *Poems of the Dragonfly* was the French poet Stéphane Mallarmé. Mallarmé later wrote a famous poem called *A Throw of the Dice Will Never Abolish Chance* (*Un Coup de dés jamais n'abolira le hasard*), a highly avant-garde experiment that was acclaimed by French critics. The text in this poem grows larger and smaller, is widely spaced on the page, and is generally arranged with the same design sensibility as Japanese *chirashigaki*. In other words, when something the Japanese had been doing for more than a thousand years was executed for the first time in French, people took it as cutting-edge and experimental. This illustrates how major its Japanese characteristics were.

Word and Image in Comics

We can also see the union of word and image in comics. Figure 55 is *Sweet Dreams, Baby!*, a painting by Roy Lichtenstein based on American popular cartoons. The text "Pow" is a sound effect, of course. Searching for a Japanese example, I looked through a manga that my children used to read, *The Circuit Wolf* (*Sākitto no ōkami*), and found many sound effects for revving and zooming cars in angular katakana. These were stylized to be even spikier than usual—the shape indicates the ferocity of the sound. This is seen in Western comics, too: a large "Blam!" when someone fires a pistol, and so on. But in Japan, kana can represent not only sounds but also actions or events that make no sound at all. This often confuses overseas readers.

For example, figure 56 is a panel from *The Circuit Wolf* that contains a large "*Pita!*" (ピタッ) in katakana. Instead of sound, this represents action—to be specific, a sudden stop. This is common in Japanese manga. Figure

Figure 55. Roy Lichtenstein, *Sweet Dreams, Baby!*, 1965. Ōhara Museum of Art.
© Estate of Roy Lichtenstein, New York & JASPAR, Tokyo, 2017.

Figure 56. Ikezawa Satoshi, *The Circuit Wolf* (*Sākitto no ōkami*) (excerpt). Shūeisha, *Shōnen Jump* magazine.

Figure 57. Maya Mineo, *Patalliro!* (*Patariro*) (excerpt). Hakusensha.

Figure 58. Ishinomori Shōtarō, *Dragon God Pond* (*Ryūjin numa*) (excerpt), 1961. Kōdansha, *Shōjo Club* magazine.

57 is from Maya Mineo's *Patalliro!*, another from my daughter's old collection. The text in these panels reads "*Sū*" (スウ) and "*Suru suru suru*" (スル スルスル), representing the action of slipping out of bed and flying away.

Finally, consider figure 58, a panel from Ishinomori Shōtarō's *Dragon God Pond* (*Ryūjin numa*). The text reads "*Shiin*" (シーン) and is quite untranslatable: it represents silence itself. Manga are popular around the world, and many of Ishinomori's works are available in other languages, but this *shiin* is something that cannot be translated. In other countries, text is fundamentally for representing sound; it cannot represent its absence. I understand that even the Korean translation could not accommodate this *shiin*. Apparently, translations usually just delete the characters entirely. It can be understood from the image alone that the scene is quiet, of course, but in Japan text is also used in this highly artful way. Japan is truly distinctive.

It seems that there is something—call it a bodily sense—peculiar to the Japanese people which allows sounds to express the soundless. In Kabuki, for example, the *taiko* drum is used to represent snow. Unlike in a battle scene, where the *taiko* is struck fiercely, in scenes with falling snow it is tapped lightly and repeatedly. This is strange, because on a night when snow is falling, there is no sound at all. But this atmosphere is evoked by the sound of the drum, something like the *shiin* seen above. The Japanese can sense this; that is the Japanese sensibility, and it is not found outside Japan. In other countries, sound effects in plays are all representations of actual sounds.

Poems and Pictures Today

And this use of text has continued in Japan to the present day. Figure 59 is "The Plum's Perfume Fills the Air as Snow Falls," a print by Munakata Shikō incorporating a passage from Yanagi Sōetsu's *Poems from the Heart* (*Kokorouta*). The calligraphy and image are both by Munakata. He is also famous for his series of prints made in collaboration with Yoshii Isamu, which includes poems such as:

ka ni kaku ni	how, oh how
Gion wa koishi	I long for Gion—
neru toki mo	even at night
makura no shita o	beneath my pillow
mizu no nagaruru	the water flows

This came about because Munakata was good friends with Yoshii; he collected 31 of Yoshii's poems and created a series of prints called *Wandering Away from Home* (*Ryūrishō*) of them. Again, the imagery, coloring, and text were all done by Munakata himself.

This work was well received, and before long the writer Tanizaki Jun'ichirō proposed a joint project to Munakata as well. Another set of prints resulted, one of which had the poem:

ishidan o	counting as she
kazoete noboru	climbs the stairs of stone

Figure 59. Munakata Shikō, "The Plum's Perfume Fills the Air as Snow Falls" (Ume kaorimitsu yuki furu mo) from *Poems from the Heart* (*Kokorouta hanga-saku*), 1958. Ōhara Museum of Art.

Figure 60. Munakata Shikō, "Three Sisters" (San shimai no saku) from *Poems by Tanizaki Jun'ichirō* (*Utauta hanga-saku*). 1956. Ōhara Museum of Art. (See plate 11)

otomego no	a young girl
sode ni chiri kuru	on whose sleeve alight
yamazakura kana	the mountain cherry blossoms

The poem is Tanizaki's own, and his name is written in the painting too. Tanizaki actually had a very modern sensibility, as can be seen in figure 60, which includes this poem:

sannin no	three sisters
ane to imōto	older and younger
inarabite	stand together
shashin torasu nari	to take a photograph
Kintaikyō no ue	on Kintai Bridge

Thus, even in the postwar period, the connection between poems and calligraphy remained part of Japan's aesthetic consciousness.

II

Japanese Beauty, Western Beauty

East Meets West: Forms of Expression in Japanese and Western Art

The Discovery of Japan's Aesthetic Consciousness

In an interview with Claude Monet published in the June 1909 issue of the *Gazette des beaux-arts*, the renowned painter of water lilies makes his affinity for Japanese art clear:

> If you absolutely must … find an affiliation for me, put me with the Japanese of old: the refinement of their taste has always appealed to me, and I approve of the suggestions of their aesthetic, which evokes the presence by the shadow, the whole by the fragment.

The influx of Japanese art into Europe in the latter half of the nineteenth century is well known. Ukiyo-e, paintings on folding screens, illustrated books, ceramics, and even furniture: imported from Japan in great quantities, these artworks not only aroused the interest of collectors and connoisseurs but also influenced the forms employed by a new generation of painters, particularly impressionists like Monet and Manet. In Monet's celebrated *La Japonaise*, he simply experimented with painting a French woman (his wife Camille, in fact) in a kimono, but as the interview above shows, his interest in Japanese art was motivated by more than just exoticism. Rather, he perceived a similarity between the forms of expression characteristic of Japanese art and the work he was producing himself.

Monet was not alone in extolling the newly discovered aesthetic consciousness of Japanese art. The French critic Ernest Chesneau was one of the first to take a serious interest in the art of Japan, identifying asymmetry, stylization, and polychromatism as its three basic characteristics in an 1869 lecture. In his 1878 essay "Le Japon à Paris," he argued that the passion among artists and connoisseurs for Japanese art was rooted in admiration for "the unexpectedness of its compositions, the science of its forms, the richness of its tone, the originality of its pictorial effects, and at the same time the simplicity of the means employed to obtain these results." Painters as diverse as Degas, Van Gogh, Gauguin, Toulouse-Lautrec, and even Bonnard cherished the art of Japan for more than just the foreignness in its peculiar motifs—although that was undeniably part of the appeal. They admired it for its refined stylization, as the many new forms of artistic expression appearing at that time show. Clearly, the Westerners who embraced the art of Japan saw something in it that had been absent from the mainstream of their own tradition up until that time.

The Introduction of Western Painting Techniques to Japan

In exactly the same way, when Western art was introduced to Japan in the eighteenth century, largely in the form of prints and illustrations in books, Japanese artists who were fortunate enough to encounter such works admired the realism of their perspective and shading—techniques not used in traditional Japanese art—and diligently set about mastering them.

Japan's contact with the Western world dates back to the arrival of Christian missionaries in the sixteenth century, primarily from Spain and Portugal. Figure 1 is an example of a seventeenth-century genre that came to be known as *nanban-byōbu*: painted screens depicting "southern barbarians," as Westerners were called at the time. On the left, a European ship has arrived at harbor; on the right are the Europeans themselves, some newly disembarked from the ship and others waiting for them on shore. The painting technique is entirely Japanese, but the choice of foreigners as subject matter was something distinctly new.

However, Japan's honeymoon with the "southern barbarians" was brief. The Tokugawa shogunate issued edicts banning Christianity and instituting a policy of national isolation, and these cultural developments were soon all but forgotten. As a result, it was not until the second half of the

Figure 1. Kanō Sanraku (attributed), *Southern Barbarians* (*Nanban byōbu*) (right panel), Momoyama period. Suntory Museum of Art.

eighteenth century that Western artistic techniques were truly introduced to Japan.

Broadly speaking, this took place in four stages. The first stage extended from the late eighteenth century to the "opening" of Japan to the outside world in the mid-nineteenth century. This corresponds to the period of national isolation imposed by the shogunate, but, as many scholars have observed, even at this time Japan's isolation was not complete. Trade with Holland was permitted to continue, albeit in a restricted fashion, through the port of Nagasaki in Kyushu. Driven by curiosity and intellectual fervor, pioneers like Odano Naotake and Shiba Kōkan obtained books and prints from this source and learned the techniques of Western art from them. These artists also developed an interest in other aspects of Western society, and their activities were intimately connected to the intellectual movement known as "Dutch Learning" (*Rangaku*)—a sizeable network of people in scholarly, literary, and technical fields gathering and exchanging information from and about the West, as filtered through the Netherlands, Japan's sole European trading partner at the time.

Odano Naotake is perhaps best known today as the painter of the masterpiece *Shinobazu Pond* (p. 135), but he was also involved in the production of one of Japan's first Western-style anatomy texts, the *New Anatomy* (fig. 2), translated from the Dutch and published in 1774. Naotake drew as many as twenty pages of detailed anatomical illustrations for the book.

He also drew its cover—basically a faithful imitation of the Dutch original, but with a number of intriguing changes to avoid trouble from the censors, like the repositioned left hand on the male figure.

The second stage of the introduction of Western art to Japan lasted roughly twenty years, beginning with the arrival of the US fleet under Commodore Perry in 1854 and the forced signing of trade treaties with the European powers shortly afterwards. These were turbulent decades, extending through the fall of the Tokugawa shogunate to the early years of the Meiji period, but enterprising Japanese people were able to make direct if extremely limited contact with Westerners. Some artists even traveled to Europe to study Western art at its birthplace. Takahashi Yuichi, painter of *Salmon* (fig. 3), was one of the most accomplished among this generation of Western-style Japanese artists, although he himself never went further afield than Shanghai.

The third stage lasted for another twenty years, beginning with the 1876 founding of the Technical Fine Art School attached to the Imperial College of Engineering in Tokyo. Three Italian artists were invited to teach at the school, making it possible for the first time to receive a systematic artistic education from Western instructors without leaving Japan. Of the three, it was Antonio Fontanesi, a former professor at the Accademia Albertina in Turin recommended by the Italian government, whose lectures would have the most decisive impact on the development of Western-style art in Japan. Fontanesi spent just two years in the country, and the Technical Fine Art School itself was closed in 1883, but his influence is

Left: Figure 2. Odano Naotake, *New Anatomy (Kaitai shinsho)* (cover), 1774.

Right: Figure 3. Takahashi Yuichi, *Salmon (Sake)*, 1887. Tokyo University of the Arts.

apparent in the work of Japanese artists for many years afterwards. Compare the example of Fontanesi's work in figure 4 with *Cherry Trees in Sendai* (fig. 5) by Koyama Shōtarō, one of his students.

The fourth and final stage of Western art's introduction to Japan began in 1896, when Kuroda Seiki accepted a professorial position in the Tokyo School of Fine Arts' newly created Department of Western-Style Painting, which had been founded as a successor to the Technical Fine Art School in 1887. Kuroda had studied art for nine years in France, producing works such as *Reading* (fig. 6) and *Chrysanthemums and Western Ladies* (*Kikuka to seiyō fujin*). The former was particularly admired, even being selected for exhibition at the salon of the Société des artistes français. Kuroda broke entirely with the tradition maintained by Fontanesi's pupils, championing a new style that eventually came to dominate the mainstream of Western-style Japanese art.

In this way, over the course of more than a century, the distance between Japan and the West was gradually reduced. At each stage of the process, Japanese artists adopted ideas from a different Western country, with each choice reflecting the historical circumstances at the time.

During the first stage, the most important country for Western art enthusiasts was the Netherlands, Japan's sole Western trading partner. Like other intellectuals and scientists of the time, artists strove to acquire "Dutch Learning" about the history and culture of the West. The second stage began when the United States and United Kingdom forced Japan to open its

Figure 4. Antonio Fontanesi,
Cows in the Meadow, ca. 1867.
Tokyo University of the Arts.

Figure 5. Koyama Shōtarō, *Cherry Trees in Sendai* (*Sendai no sakura*), 1881.
Niigata Prefectural Museum of Modern Art.

Figure 6. Kuroda Seiki,
Reading (*Dokusho*), 1890–1891.
Tokyo National Museum.
Image: TNM Image Archives.
(See plate 12)

ports, and the influence of those two countries remained preeminent. One of the most prominent intellectuals of the period, Fukuzawa Yukichi, quickly began studying English after visiting Yokohama to find it full of signage in that language rather than the Dutch he had learned in Osaka.

The pivot from Dutch to English encapsulates the changes in how Western culture was received in Japan during this period, and this was no less true for the art world. Takahashi Yuichi, mentioned above as the painter of *Salmon*, learned oil painting from Charles Wirgman, a correspondent for the *Illustrated London News*. One of Takahashi's fellow painters, Kunisawa Shinkurō, studied art in London from 1870 through 1874 before returning home and opening the Shōgidō, the first private school in Japan to teach the techniques of Western art. Lectures at the Shōgidō were largely based on Japanese translations of books on artistic technique that Kunisawa had brought back with him from England, including everything from anatomy manuals to theoretical treatises on landscape and portrait painting. The most noteworthy among these materials was the *Discourses* of Sir Joshua Reynolds. Translated into Japanese in 1890, this book was the first opportunity Japanese readers had to learn about the re-nowned English painter.

By the dawn of the third stage, it was Italy that was viewed as most central to art, as the Technical Fine Art School's employment of three pro-fessors from that country might suggest. Fontanesi's lectures, too, focused chiefly on Italian artists like Tiziano, Tintoretto, and Guido Reni. It was not until the fourth stage, when Kuroda Seiki rose to prominence, that the Western-style artists of Japan, like the artists of the West at the time, be-gan to view France and particularly Paris as the center of the art world.

Throughout all four stages, but particularly in the first two, what most interested Japanese artists about Western art were its techniques of repro-ducing what was actually seen. Admiration for the illusion of a perfect three-dimensional world on a flat surface is readily apparent in *Discussion of Western Art* (*Seiyōga dan*), published in 1799 by Shiba Kōkan, a gifted artist and one of those most interested in the West at the time.

> Japanese and Chinese techniques are incapable of depicting truth. When depicting something rounded, they simply draw a circle and call it the shape of a bullet. They cannot show that the center pro-trudes. Even drawing a portrait from the front, one cannot depict the central prominence of the nose. Drawing arose not from brush-work but from the shadows cast by the sun.

Of course, the flaws Shiba Kōkan laments—flatness, forms with no sense of three-dimensionality, colors without shading—were precisely the fea-tures that animated the enthusiasm for *japonisme* in Europe. Japan and the West were fascinated by each other's art out of more than mutual exoti-cism: each tradition employed forms of artistic expression that were entire-ly new to the other.

Two Forms of Expression

The best way to understand the differences between these forms of expres-sion is by example. Figure 7 is a work by Kitagawa Utamaro, while figure 8 is Leonardo da Vinci's *Mona Lisa*. Both are portraits of female figures,

Left: Figure 7. Kitagawa Utamaro, *Geisha of the West District (Saigoku no geisha)*.

Right: Figure 8. Leonardo da Vinci, *Mona Lisa*, 1503–1519. Louvre Museum.

but where the *Mona Lisa* perfectly creates the illusion of a three-dimensional world, Utamaro's work shows no sign any such modeling. In fact, it contains no shading whatsoever.

Figures 9 and 10 both depict a female figure from behind, her face reflected in a mirror. The two works are so utterly alike in composition that a viewer might suspect some connection between them, but they employ entirely different forms of expression. In his charming portrait of young Antoinette Herbert, currently in the collection of a private museum in Japan, Jean-François Millet includes the background in full detail, including the stately sofa, the elaborate ornamentation of the mirror frame, and the luxurious curtains. Utamaro's composition, however, banishes all secondary motifs to concentrate solely on the main subjects: the woman and her mirror. Similarly, he uses absolutely no modeling or shading. The woman's face is represented only by its outline, with no attempt to capture any shadows or highlights as in Millet's portrait of Antoinette. Nevertheless, Utamaro successfully creates a highly refined and elegant composition.

In his 1436 treatise *On Painting* (*Della pittura/De pictura*), Florentine polymath Leon Battista Alberti wrote:

> I almost always view as mediocre that painter who does not understand well the strength of each shadow and the lights on each surface. I praise, with the consent of both the learned and the ignorant, those faces that, as if they were sculpted, seem to come forth from

Left: Figure 9. Jean-François Millet, *Antoinette Herbert Looking in the Mirror* (*Antoinette Hébert devant le miroir*), ca. 1844–1845. Murauchi Art Museum.

Right: Figure 10. Kitagawa Utamaro, *Naniwa Okita Admiring Herself in a Mirror* (*Sugatami shichinin keshō*). Metropolitan Museum of Art. (See plate 13)

Figure 12. Jean-Antoine Watteau, *The Dance* (*La danse*), ca. 1719. Gemäldegalerie, Berlin.

Figure 11. Anonymous, *Dance* (*Butō-zu*), seventeenth century. Suntory Museum of Art.

the painting; and on the contrary I criticize those faces in which no art shines except perhaps that of drawing.

Had Alberti been familiar with works like Utamaro's, he might have expressed a slightly different view.

The Aesthetics of Omission and the Close-Up

The next two works depict dancing, again with utterly different forms of expression. The most striking thing about figure 11, a seventeenth-century Japanese painting, is the artist's bold elimination of everything but the central figure. The dancer's kimono is depicted in meticulous detail, but there is no hint of background or scene. We cannot even tell if the dancer is indoors or outdoors.

In Jean-Antoine Watteau's fascinating, perfectly executed *The Dance* (fig. 12), however, we grasp the dancer's surroundings at a glance. The pastoral nature of the scene is obvious from the shepherd boys admiring the dancing woman and attempting to play the flute for her, along with other skillfully shaded detail.

As the earlier example from Utamaro also demonstrated, Japanese artists tended to eliminate elements deemed secondary or otherwise unnecessary to focus solely on the primary motif—an "aesthetics of omission." Sakai Hōitsu's *Flowering Plants of Summer and Autumn* (fig. 13) is another excellent example of this. In a Western work like Constable's *Stratford Mill* (fig. 14), the artist recreates everything found in nature—the clouds, the sunlight on the ground, the river, the rocks and trees, and so on—to create a landscape that appears entire and whole before the viewer. Hōitsu's *Flowering Plants*, however, includes nothing but its two main motifs. The grasses and plants are drawn in the finest detail, but placed in the extreme foreground of the picture; apart from some rather stylized running water (viewed, incidentally, from above) in the upper right, the work contains nothing else at all. There is no ground, no meadow, no sky—just a uniform silver background.

The same pattern is visible in the next two examples, which take trees as their theme: *Cypress Tree* (fig. 15), attributed to sixteenth-century Japanese painter Kanō Eitoku, and Dutch painter Meindert Hobbema's *The Avenue at Middelharnis* (fig. 16). Here, too, the Japanese work has a pure gold background. The upper parts of the tree trunks are painted as if cut off by the edge of the frame rather than intentionally left out by the artist. This "close-up" effect was popular among Japanese artists and shows another aspect of the aesthetics of omission. As can be seen in the many illustrations of episodes from the *Tale of Genji*, artists loyal to this aesthetic did not hesitate to omit even the ceiling and roof when depicting an indoor scene (fig. 17). This was known as the "roofless house" (*fukinuki-yatai*) technique, unique to Japanese art and developed to show indoor scenes without interference from irrelevant obstacles. The peculiarity of this approach is even more apparent by comparison with the perfectly de-

Figure 13. Sakai Hōitsu, *Flowering Plants of Summer and Autumn* (*Natsu-aki kusa-zu byōbu*), ca. 1821. Tokyo National Museum.

Figure 14. John Constable, *Stratford Mill*, ca. 1820. London National Gallery.

Figure 15. Kanō Eitoku, *Cypress Tree* (*Hinoki-zu byōbu*), 1590. Tokyo National Museum.

Right: Figure 16. Meindert Hobbema, *The Avenue at Middelharnis* (*Het laantje van Middelharnis*), 1689. London National Gallery.

Bottom left: Figure 17. Anonymous, "Yūgiri" from *Illustrations from the Tale of Genji* (*Genji Monogatari zue*), twelfth century. Gotoh Museum.

Bottom right: Figure 18. Diego Velázquez, *The Ladies-in-Waiting* (*Las meninas*), 1656. Museo del Prado.

picted rooms in works like Diego Velázquez's masterpiece *The Ladies-in-Waiting* (fig. 18).

Moving on to cityscapes, figure 19 is a folding screen painting in the "In and around the capital" (*rakuchū rakugai*) genre that flourished in sixteenth- and seventeenth-century Japan, while figure 20 is *View of Delft* by the seventeenth-century Dutch painter Johannes Vermeer. Vermeer's com-

Figure 19. Kanō Eitoku, *Scenes In and Around Kyoto* (*Rakuchū rakugai-zu byōbu*)—Uesugi screens, Muromachi period. Yonezawa City Uesugi Museum. (See plate 14)

Figure 20. Johannes Vermeer, *View of Delft* (*Gezicht op Delft*), ca. 1660–1661. Mauritshuis.

Figure 21. Yasui Sōtarō, *Nude (Rafuzō)*.

Figure 22. Sketch by Henri de Toulouse-Lautrec.

position employs geometrical perspective, as if we were standing in a fixed position overlooking the town. The Japanese painting, on the other hand, is covered in buildings and other structures, with golden clouds scattered throughout that give a sense of looking down on the city from above. Where Vermeer's work implies three-dimensional depth, the screen painting conveys a sense of two-dimensional flatness.

In *On Painting*, Alberti writes that "in a painting, surfaces appear most brilliant and resplendent when they have the same proportion of white to black as of light to shadow in the things themselves." If this is so, monochrome drawings should be where the differences between Japanese and Western forms of representation are most pronounced. Figure 21 is a sketch of a nude done in complete accordance with the traditions of Western Academism. The dark background and meticulously drawn shadows emphasize the roundedness of each part of the body, and the study has an overall realism that evokes a living human being. Figure 22, however, does not use shading in this way. Instead, plain, fast, and free brush-strokes evoke a simple rustic world: a mountain and river, a boat, a fisherman in traditional Japanese rain gear, and a net in the water.

In this case, however, the sketch in Japanese style is actually the work of French painter Henri de Toulouse-Lautrec, while the Western-style nude was drawn by the Japanese artist Yasui Sōtarō, who studied at the Académie Julian in Paris in the early twentieth century.

Contrasting Principles

Underlying the differences between Western and Japanese approaches to representation are two fundamentally contrasting sets of basic principles.

Western art, at least until the rise of Manet and the other impressionists in the second half of the nineteenth century, adhered to the tradition of realism established during the Renaissance. Alberti's *On Painting* says:

> The role of the painter is to draw and color all the bodies given to him, with lines and colors, on a surface, such that from a certain distance and at a certain position relative to the center, the painted things one sees appear prominent and very similar to the given bodies.

Alberti is speaking of the recreation of a three-dimensional space within a two-dimensional picture through techniques like perspective, modeling, and shading. A good example of this from a near-contemporary of Alberti is Rogier van der Weyden's *Saint Luke Drawing the Virgin* (fig. 23). Perspective lends depth to the space depicted, while a sense of volume is conveyed through modeling, shading, and judicious use of shadow. These were the basic techniques used by painters to create the illusion of three-dimensionality on a flat plane.

As another example, consider *Portrait of a Young Man* (fig. 24) by Jan

Left: Figure 23. Rogier van der Weyden, *Saint Luke Drawing the Virgin* (*Lucas schildert de Madonna*), 1435–1440. Museum of Fine Arts, Boston.

Right: Figure 24. Jan van Eyck, *Portrait of a Man ("Léal Souvenir")*, 1432. London National Gallery.

van Eyck, another painter from the same period. Not only does Van Eyck successfully reproduce his model's outward appearance, the text at the bottom of the painting looks almost exactly as if it were really carved into stone. Blurring the boundary between reality and reproduction through illusion in this way had been viewed as fundamental to painting since ancient times. In his work *Images* (*Imagines*), the ancient Greek writer Philostratus describes a picture of Narcissus he saw in Naples as follows:

> The painting is highly realistic, showing even the dew dripping from the flowers and the bee perched atop them. Whether a real bee is deceived into visiting a painted flower, or whether we are deceived into believing that a painted bee is real, I do not know.

The famous competition between Zeuxis and Parrhasius in Pliny the Elder's *Natural History* (*Naturalis historia*) is another example from the ancient world:

> [Parrhasius] is recorded to have entered into a competition with Zeuxis, who produced a picture of some grapes so realistic that birds flew into the building; upon which the other [Parrhasius] drew a picture of a curtain so realistic that Zeuxis, excited by the verdict of the birds, demanded that the curtain be drawn and the picture displayed; and, realizing his mistake, conceded the palm with a praiseworthy modesty, saying that he might have deceived the birds, but Parrhasius had deceived a painter.

None of these works survive today. (In fact, the picture of Narcissus that Philostratus describes in such detail probably never existed at all.) Clearly, however, Philostratus and Pliny saw painting as an art not just of representation but also of deception, just like Alberti and other Western painters after them. The techniques invented by Western artists were extremely effective for realizing this ideal.

Japanese artists, by contrast, never sought to recreate a three-dimensional world through illusion. On the contrary, they respected the planarity of the medium and came to emphasize it strongly. They did strive to recreate the real world in their work, but their approach to this goal was entirely different.

Figure 25 is another painting in the "In and around the capital" genre. The ornamental and formalized nature of the work is obvious, but does not impede its ability to suggest space or spatial composition. The screens depict a complex but clear spatial composition covering the entire city, incorporating countless temples, palace buildings, and other structures in their correct positional relationships. If the goal is to convey both the external appearance of a city and the respective locations of its various buildings, a planar map is more effective than a picture postcard. Japanese folding

Figure 25.
Iwasa Matabei
(attributed), *Scenes
In and Around Kyoto
(Rakuchū rakugai-zu
byōbu)*—Funaki screens
(left screen, detail),
seventeenth century.
Tokyo National Museum.

screen paintings like this represented cities in a manner entirely unlike Western realism but no less rational. The fundamental difference between the two approaches is the point from which each subject is viewed.

Western techniques like perspective and shading are premised on capturing an image like a photograph. The scene is depicted at a specific moment and from a fixed point of view. The distances between the painter and the subjects of the painting are represented through variation in form and color—dark versus light tones, warm versus cool colors, and so on. Figures in the foreground are painted much larger than those in the background, but this does not imply anything about the size of the actual people in the scene. Similarly, if the clothing of the figures in the background is drawn more vaguely, this does not signify that their clothing is inferior or soiled. Realistic effects cannot be produced without such understandings.

If the painter were to change position, all the spatial relationships in the picture would change accordingly. If, before painting each figure in the painting, the painter moved to stand right in front of their model, all would be equally large and equally distinct in the finished work. The effect of perspective would be prevented from arising.

This is exactly the approach taken by painters of "In and around the capital" works in Japan. The painter moves freely through the town, observing the shops and people, drawing them in detail based on close examination, so that they are lined up side by side on the folding screen. Put another way, instead of cityscapes as viewed from a single fixed point, these works depict each part of the city viewed from a different vantage point. Each element is drawn as vividly as the next, right down to the details of faces and clothing, and the overall impression is one of flatness, with no sense of distance between the things depicted.

The artist's free-roaming viewpoint not only moves horizontally through the capital to show us each individual part, it also moves vertically to convey the nature of each place and motif as clearly as possible. The basic layout of the residential and temple architecture that constitutes urban Kyoto is viewed from on high; we know from our own everyday experiences that this is the best way to convey the spatial composition of a city. But the façade of each individual building is viewed from street level, as are the people passing by.

Figure 26. Anonymous, "*Suzumushi* (Bell Crickets) II" from *Illustrated Handscroll of The Tale of Genji* (*Genji Monogatari emaki*), twelfth century. Gotoh Museum.

Figure 27. Suzuki Harunobu, *Kasamori O-Sen*, eighteenth century. Tokyo National Museum.

Freely moving points of view are very common in Japanese art. To give just two examples, consider figures 26 and 27. The former is an indoor scene from the twelfth-century *Illustrated Handscroll of the Tale of Genji*. The setting is drawn from above, but the characters are viewed from a normal, horizontal vantage point. Figure 27 is an elegant and fascinating ukiyo-e by Suzuki Harunobu from the late eighteenth century, depicting a teahouse that stood by the entrance to Kasamori Shrine in Edo. The teahouse was famous as the place of employment of a woman named O-Sen, one of the "three great beauties" of the age. O-Sen is at the center of the frame, and, like the customers and the other employee, is viewed from street level. However, in the background, only the lower part of the torii symbolizing the entrance to the shrine is shown above the diagonally drawn flagstones. The artist's skillful combination of these elements preserves the harmony of the composition despite the difference in vantage points.

Techniques thus arose within Japanese art that were entirely different from those of the Western Renaissance tradition, with artists learning how best to arrange depictions of multiple objects viewed from a free-roaming point of view. But while the vantage point's movement was free, it was not arbitrary. Rather, artists adopted the most appropriate viewpoint for each object: the city as a whole from above, human figures from the side, and scenes of city life in close-up. Arranging the objects of a painting side-by-side like this makes it impossible to use the rules of perspective to indicate distance by drawing things smaller or more faintly. Instead, it emphasizes the spread of the painting across the folding screen. Where Western art emphasizes horizontal depth with respect to the canvas, Japanese art is characterized by parallel planarity.

These different forms of representation represent different artistic philosophies. Western art assumes an absolute *subject*—the painter, for our purposes—to whose viewpoint everything else is subordinated. In the Japanese tradition, the opposite is true: *objects* are prioritized, and the most appropriate viewpoint is adopted for each one. This mirrors the linearity of Western thought, in which a unitary center is viewed as the absolute value, versus the multi-dimensionality of Japanese culture, which accepts the co-existence of mutually inconsistent values as easily as the coexistence of multiple vantage points in a single painting.

Design in Japanese Art

A fondness for ornamental effect is often apparent in Japanese art. Techniques like covering background details with a gold field, however, are more than just a decorative luxury. They are also deeply connected with two of Japanese art's unique characteristics: planarity and simplicity of composition. A gold field not only prevents the viewer from entering into the depths of the scene, it also conceals unnecessary details that would otherwise distract from the main motifs.

The left half of Tawaraya Sōtatsu's *Bugaku Dancers* (fig. 28) depicts only the lower part of a pine tree and six performers. In Ogata Kōrin's *Irises* (p. 77), the lushly blooming flowers of the title stand utterly alone. A painting of the same subject in the tradition of Western realism would also show the surface of the pond in which the irises bloom, as well as the sky and other background details. Kōrin boldly excises such secondary elements, covering the entire background with a flat gold field. The result is surprisingly voluptuous given its simplicity. The same aesthetics of omission are on display in the *Frolicking Animals* (*Chōjū giga*) scrolls of Kōsanji Temple and Hasegawa Tōhaku's famous ink wash painting *Pine Trees* (p. 161).

The renowned sixteenth-century tea-ceremony master Sen no Rikyū was another proponent of the aesthetics of omission. Rikyū's garden was known to be full of a rare and beautiful type of morning glory. When his lord Toyotomi Hideyoshi asked to see them, Rikyū invited Hideyoshi to visit him. The appointed morning was fine and sunny, but Hideyoshi arrived at Rikyū's residence to find the garden bare: the morning glories had all been plucked. Hideyoshi was furious, but when Rikyū ushered him into the tea-ceremony room, he became transfixed by the decoration Rikyū had prepared for the *tokonoma* alcove: a single morning glory blossom. Hideyoshi returned home entirely satisfied.

The Japanese aesthetic consciousness has an undeniable soft spot for the gorgeous and ornamental. But as this tale shows, the ideal is not to simply revel in abundance. Rather, such effects are deployed with a simplifying element of restraint, excising whatever is unnecessary.

Kōrin's *Red and White Plum Blossoms* (fig. 29) exemplifies all the elements of Japanese aesthetics discussed so far. Its use of rich color on a gold field has high ornamental value. In excluding the ground, the sky, and the surrounding grasslands to show only the three main motifs, it demonstrates the aesthetics of omission—and upon close examination, those three motifs are clearly depicted from different viewpoints, the trees horizontally and the river from overhead. Finally, the aesthetics of the close-up are evident in the white-blossomed plum tree on the left, of which only the roots and the tips of the bowed branches are visible.

Figure 28.
Tawaraya Sōtatsu,
Bugaku Dancers Screens
(*Bugaku-zu byōbu*),
seventeenth century.
Daigoji Temple.
(See plate 15)

Two different forms of expression; two different traditions. What form did their meeting take? The work of Shiba Kōkan is an instructive example from the Japanese side. As noted earlier, Kōkan was one of his age's most fervent admirers of Western civilization in Japan. Originally trained in traditional Japanese forms of expression, he later came to favor the Western approach so strongly that he dismissed the techniques of Japanese art as "child's play."

The first Western medium Kōkan turned his hand to was the copperplate print. His 1794 print *Art Studio* (fig. 30) is proudly captioned (in Chinese) "Made in Japan—Shiba Kōkan." A painter at his easel stands at the center of the frame, and the paraphernalia piled up around him, including books, a globe, a compass, a printing press, and experimental equipment, hints at the intellectual nature of artistic endeavor.

Surprisingly, Kōkan also produced an oil painting of the Zeuxis episode mentioned earlier. The work is now sadly lost, surviving only in the form of an old photograph taken before World War II (fig. 31). The scene depicted is Zeuxis's atelier. On a platform stands a painting of a bunch of grapes, which two birds who have flown in through the window attempt to eat as Zeuxis and two others look on in astonishment. Kōkan's boundless admiration for Western culture can be seen in the signature on the painting, which

Figure 29. Ogata Kōrin, *Red and White Plum Blossoms* (*Kōhakubai-zu byōbu*), eighteenth century. MOA Museum of Art.

is in Dutch this time: "Kookan Schildert, A.D. 1789." In placing this signature at the bottom of Zeuxis's painting, Kōkan was no doubt expressing his determination to follow in the proud footsteps of the ancient realist.

Despite his devotion to the Western tradition, however, Kōkan was unable to entirely eliminate his unconscious Japanese sensitivities. Figure 32 shows another of his works, a picture of a Western couple. Their clothing and accessories are unmistakably of the West, but the composition with the tree behind them is in accordance with his native tradition. Even the vertical shape of the painting recalls a Japanese hanging scroll.

Kōkan produced several studies of this work before executing the final version, and these studies actually follow their Western model more closely. In the background of one study (fig. 33), instead of a tree there is a Western-style building, complete with Dutch sign; another, still earlier study (fig. 34) has a less vertical form factor, and the depiction of the Western—specifically, Dutch—buildings in the background emphasizes depth of field rather than planarity.

Apart from the rather distinctive Japanese-style brushwork and Kōkan's signature, these studies contain no Japanese elements at all; without the signature, they would probably be assumed the work of a Western artist. And no wonder: Kōkan was in fact faithfully copying a copperplate

Figure 30. Shiba Kōkan,
Art Studio (*Gashitsu-zu*), 1794.
Kobe City Museum.

Figure 31. Shiba Kōkan,
Zeuxis and the Birds
(*Zeukushisu to kotori*).

Figure 32. Shiba Kōkan, *Foreign Landscape and Figures* (*Ijin fūkei jinbutsuga*), 1789–1801. Kobe City Museum.

Figure 33. Shiba Kōkan, *Sailor* (*Sen'in-zu*).

Figure 34. Shiba Kōkan, *Sailor* (*Sen'in-zu*), 1785.

Figure 35. Jan and Caspar Luyken, "Sailor" (Zeeman) from *The Book of Trades* (*Het Menselyk Bedryf*).

Figure 36. Shiba Kōkan,
The Cooper (Taruzukuri), 1793–1796.
Tokyo National Museum.

print in a book he owned (fig. 35): the *Book of Trades*, a collection of illustrations by the father-son team Jan and Caspar Luyken, published 1694 in Amsterdam. Over the course of copying and recopying this Western work, however, Kōkan instinctively gave it a Japanese composition.

Kōkan's oil painting *The Cooper* (fig. 36) offers another example of this type of conversion. This work, too, began as a diligent crib from the *Book of Trades*, but the finished oil painting is longer along the horizontal axis, as if to evoke the proportions of a folding screen. The tops of the trees are now cut off by the edge of the painting, with the tips of the branches drooping in from out of frame.

In the West, the artistic encounter with Japan gave rise to *japonisme*, a trend so well known that there is no need to recount its history here. Still, the words of Monet quoted at the beginning of this chapter are illuminating. Monet was a fervent admirer of Japanese art, and his description of an aesthetic "which evokes the presence by the shadow, the whole by the fragment" shows that he understood perfectly well what he saw in it. Observing the same sort of cross-cultural interpretation and influence in the work of Japanese artists, we can say this much for certain: the meeting of East and West was real, and the art that followed in its wake was a fusion based on genuine understanding.

The Dawn of Japanese Oil Painting

I

In December 1871, three years after the Meiji Restoration, an official Japanese mission to the United States and Europe set sail from Yokohama Bay. This major diplomatic endeavor was led by the Meiji government's recently appointed Minister of the Right, Iwakura Tomomi, in the role of Extraordinary and Plenipotentiary Ambassador. The mission visited cities across the United States before crossing to England in August 1872 to tour London and other English and European regional centers.

The official record of the mission was prepared by editor Kume Kunitake under the title *A True Account of the Ambassador Extraordinary and Plenipotentiary's Journey of Observation Through America and Europe* (*Tokumei zenken taishi Bei–Ō kairan jikki*). Chapter 39, "A Record of Cheshire," describes a November 7 tour of "Messrs. Minton's porcelain and earthenware works" in Stoke-on-Trent. Minton porcelain was admired at the time for its high quality, and the painstaking account of their unique manufacturing techniques includes an interesting aside on the meeting of artistic cultures:

There were in this factory two scroll-paintings which had been obtained from Japan. They had been used as specimens for the study of Japanese draughtsmanship. The Westerner's style of painting is naturally imbued with the techniques of painting in oils, and the artists had fallen into the error of putting in too much detail and had succumbed to the habit of paying attention to light and shade. So although they had done their best to imitate Japanese technique, the evidence of these ingrained habits was still there and could not be concealed. Similarly, when Japanese study Western painting techniques, they usually fail to get light and shade and perspective right.[1]

These comments not only bear witness to the influence of Japanese art on English crafts in the age of *japonisme*, they also perceptively identify the challenges of integrating ideas from a foreign culture. While no specific works or artists are mentioned, the author of this account clearly recognized "light and shade and perspective" as especially prominent aspects of Western painting that the Japanese tradition did not share.

The reception of Western art in Japan from the late eighteenth to the early twentieth century—setting aside the "Age of Barbarians" (*nanban jidai*) a century or two earlier, forcibly brought to an end by the shogunate—can be divided into four historical stages. These are described in more detail in the previous section, "East Meets West: Forms of Expression in Japanese and Western Art," but are recounted briefly below as well.

The first stage coincided with Japan's period of self-imposed national isolation, when all knowledge of Western art had to be gleaned from illustrations in imported books. Pioneers like Shiba Kōkan and Odano Naotake and Satake Shozan of the Akita *Ranga* ("Dutch painting") school overcame these limitations to absorb the techniques of the West, particularly those like shading and perspective that imparted a three-dimensionality previously unseen in Japanese art. The work and writings of these artists laid the foundations for what was to come.

The second stage began with the opening of the country in 1854 and saw the establishment of official facilities for researching and teaching Western art, such as the Painting Bureau of the shogunate's Institute for the Examination of Western Books (later renamed the Institute for Development). Japanese artists like Takahashi Yuichi and Goseda Yoshimatsu took up painting in oils, despite chronic difficulties obtaining paints, canvas, and even brushes.

The arrival of Antonio Fontanesi to teach at the Technical School of Art in 1876 inaugurated the third stage. Fontanesi himself was only in Japan for two years, but his teachings nurtured many important Western-style

Japanese painters. However, it was not long before the revival of Japanese traditions began. From its establishment in 1887, the Tokyo School of Fine Arts (now the Tokyo University of the Arts) excluded Western painting from its curriculum to focus on traditional Japanese painting techniques. Western-style paintings were debarred from exhibitions both inside and outside the school. Painters in this style, including some who had studied in Europe like Kawamura Kiyoo and Harada Naojirō, formed the Meiji Art Association (Meiji Bijutsukai) to continue their activities as Western art in Japan entered an extended winter. Finally, in 1896, the Tokyo School of Fine Arts established a department of Western art and invited Kuroda Seiki to lead it, ushering in the fourth stage.

The Japanese artists who worked in oils during the second and third of these stages strove to learn their craft while still in Japan. By analogy with *wasei eigo*, "Japan-made English," which describes words like *salaryman* whose components are English but which were created in Japan, we might call the work of these artists *wasei yuga*: "Japan-made oil paintings." Japanese journalists of the time called them the "Old School" (*kyūha*) as opposed to the "New School" (*shinpa*) centered around Kuroda Seiki.

Kuroda looms so large in the history of Western art in Japan that his New School tends to appear in dramatic close-up; the Old School, if not forgotten, becomes a rather unsubstantial presence in the narrative. In this essay, I aim to shed new light on the Old School's remarkable accomplishments and place in history.

There were some Old School painters who did study in Europe at an early stage; others, like Asai Chū, spent time in Europe later. But in order to identify what is "Japan-made," we focus here on painters who never visited the West at all. Their stories best illuminate the challenges of introducing and integrating a foreign culture.

To offer a few more caveats about Western culture and its influence on Japan in the context of this discussion: First, sweeping terms like "the West" and "Western painting" obscure much variation in content and form that arose over the course of this age of unrest and revolution. As noted earlier in this section, the first stage of Japan's reception of Western painting was the age of "Dutch Learning" (*Rangaku*), with virtually all knowledge of the West obtained through Dutch traders. But in the second stage, it was the United States and England that were most influential. Takahashi Yuichi and Goseda Yoshimatsu learned from Charles Wirgman, a reporter for the *Illustrated London News*; Kunisawa Shinkurō studied for four years in England, bringing back technical and theoretical books to use at his private art school, the Shōgidō. For example, the detailed technical work *Landscape Painting in Oil Colors* was translated into Japanese under the title *Guide to Oil Painting* (*Yuga michishirube*) by Honda Kinkichirō, who became head of the school after Kunisawa's death.[2] In the third stage, Fontanesi's native Italy was viewed as the home of Western art; in the fourth, France, where Kuroda Seiki had studied, became "the West" for Japanese painters.

Second, this was precisely the historical moment in Western art when cracks appeared in the foundation of Academism, the tradition that had underlain "Western art" since the Renaissance. While Japan was being opened by Western powers in the 1850s, Courbet and Millet were challenging the Academic school with their Realism; the opening of Japan's Technical Art School a couple of decades later coincides with the rise of the Impressionists. Academism retained a great deal of influence socially, of course, and many Japanese artists studied in that school. But as shown by the example of Kuroda Seiki's teacher, the Academic painter Raphaël Collin, the revolutionary expressive techniques of the Impressionists were being adopted even within Academism itself. The "Western painting" that Japanese artists took as their model was itself in flux.

The final thing to note is that the "realism" that Japanese painters praised as the key characteristic of Western art was different from the Realism that began with Courbet's nineteenth-century manifesto. Barbara Bertozzi, in her article "Antonio Fontanesi: His Experiences in Japan" (Antonio Fontanesi. La sua esperienza del Giappon), written for a 1997 exhibition in Turin, observes that "in Europe it was very rare for the word *realism* to be applied to Fontanesi's paintings, but in Japan his position as a master of 'realism' remains secure even today." This, she concludes, is "no doubt because in the world of Japanese oil painting at the time, the word *realism* referred not to a single form but rather the European artistic philosophy of recreating reality as accurately as possible."[3]

II

During Japan's period of national isolation, viewing a real Western oil painting was all but impossible.[4] "Western art" was known almost entirely through prints and illustrations in books. As a result, the unique characteristics that Japanese artists perceived in it were not its rich colors and textural expression but rather the techniques of "light and shade and perspective" mentioned in Kume's *True Account*—ways of expressing the solidity of the subject and the three-dimensional composition of space. Two early theoretical treatises, Satake Shozan's 1778 *Summary of the Laws of Painting* (*Gahō kōryō*) and Shiba Kōkan's 1799 *Discussion of Western Art* (*Seiyōga dan*), both argued for the superiority of Western artistic technique by invoking its ability to depict the prominence of the nose in a frontal portrait, or the difference between a circle and a sphere. These authors did have some knowledge of painting in oils, and Shozan even wrote in detail about the ingredients and composition of oil paints in *Understanding Painting and Drawing* (*Gato rikai*, another 1778 treatise), but there is no indication that he ever attempted an oil painting himself.

True oil painting learned from the Western tradition was not practiced in Japan until the second stage of its importation of Western art—not until after the Meiji Restoration in 1868, in fact. One of the earliest examples is Goseda Yoshimatsu's 1871 *Portrait of a Woman* (fig. 1), a frontal portrait

Figure 1. Goseda Yoshimatsu, *Portrait of a Woman* (*Fujinzō*), 1871. Tokyo University of the Arts.

of a woman sitting erect before a folding screen with a book open in her lap. The contours of her face are evoked with particularly skillful use of shading, demonstrating the sixteen-year-old Yoshimatsu's mastery of the modeling techniques he had learned from Wirgman. Takahashi Yuichi's well-known *Grand Courtesan* (fig. 2), which was probably painted in 1872, also conjures solidity through shading on the face, albeit with a slight lingering awkwardness. However, the clothing of Yuichi's subject is almost completely "flat," which, combined with the featureless background, precludes any sense of depth. The folding screen behind Yoshimatsu's subject has a similar effect, and in fact all Western-style portraits from this period combine superb modeling around the face with closed-off, solid backgrounds. If Western art was characterized by "light and shade and perspective"—the ability to capture both the subject's solidity and the space's three-dimensional composition—then at this point both Yuichi and Yoshimatsu were pursuing only the former. Spaces with sufficient depth to be called three-dimensional do not make their appearance in Yoshimatsu's work until after his enrolment in the Technical Art School.

We still have some of Yuichi's landscapes from the mid-1870s, including some paintings of places that he visited specifically to capture on canvas, like *Enoshima, Sagami Province* (*Sōshū Enoshima-zu*) and *Enoshima* (fig. 3). Yuichi's unwavering eye for the real is evident in these works, too, but most landscapes from this period start with tight close-ups of (parts

Figure 2. Takahashi Yuichi, *Grand Courtesan* (*Oiran*), 1872. Tokyo University of the Arts.

Figure 3. Takahashi Yuichi, *Enoshima* (*Enoshima-zu*), 1876–1877. Museum of Modern Art, Kamakura & Hayama.

of) plants or rocks in the foreground, skip the middle ground, and proceed directly to the background—the so-called "near–large, far–small" approach to composition often seen in Akita *Ranga* ("Dutch paintings") and the landscapes of Hiroshige. It is only after contact with Fontanesi that spaces depicted continuously from far to near from a unified viewpoint begin to appear.

Yuichi's work is notable for the unblinking observation of each subject's presence underlying his reproduction of its form. This quality is most visible in his still life paintings. In *Grand Courtesan*, his sharp observational eye and sensitive expressive ability can already be seen in the tortoiseshell comb his subject wears, the many pins and *kanzashi* (ornaments) in her hair, and the dotted *tegara* tying the entire arrangement together, but in his paintings of kitchen items or other everyday motifs, Yuichi's unsparing eye for detail and texture set him apart from his peers. In *Tofu* (fig. 4), the difference in texture between raw, grilled, and fried tofu is almost tangible, while in *Cod and Plum Blossoms* (p. 132), the fraying of the rope around the fish is drawn so exquisitely the viewer can all but feel it. In the Important Cultural Property *Salmon* (p. 91), it is the moist rawness of the partly cut away salmon and the solid presence of the rope from which it hangs that impress. But although each individual subject feels vividly present, the space they share is far less clearly conveyed. This is partly because each subject is depicted as if in extreme close-up, but also because the ele-

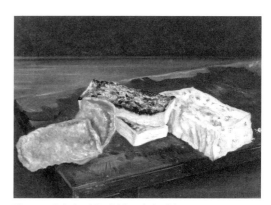

Figure 4. Takahashi Yuichi, *Tofu* (*Tōfu*), 1876–1877. Kotohiragū Shrine.

vated viewpoint in works like *Tofu* and *Cod and Plum Blossoms* creates a composition in which every part of every subject is roughly the same distance from the painter's eye. As a result, while each part is depicted in minute detail, expression of depth with respect to the frame tends to be excluded. The frame, in other words, is flattened. This is particularly unmistakable in paintings like *Rolled Cloth* (fig. 5), in which the frame is filled with rolls of cloth sitting in their open wrappers and viewed from overhead. In *Salmon*, because the background is blocked by boards, the frame has no depth to begin with.

Figure 5.
Takahashi Yuichi,
Rolled Cloth (*Makinuno*),
1873–1876. Kotohiragū
Shrine.

Figure 6.
Takahashi Yuichi,
Reader and Notebook
(*Tokuhon to sōshi*),
1875–1876.
Kotohiragū Shrine.

The lack of clarity in spatial expression is even more obvious in multiple-subject compositions like *Reader and Notebook* (fig. 6). The reader and battledore on the table are rendered as if from above, but the lamp is unmistakably shown from below. The multiple viewpoints that coexist in the work preclude any clear definition of the relative positions of the lamp, the hanging notebook, and the objects on the table. Put another way, the spatial relationships of the objects depicted are extremely vague, despite—or perhaps *because of*—the extreme detail in the depiction of each individual object.

And yet this is exactly what makes Yuichi's early still life paintings so unique and appealing. The Western techniques of perspective view all subjects from a single vantage point, calculating distances and relationships accordingly, but Yuichi's works offer a different kind of "realism"—one that rejects this fixed-viewpoint approach and abandons the sense of distance in favor of a close approach to each individual subject. The exquisite representation of detail permitted by a freely moving viewpoint and unrestrained use of the close-up, along with the flattening of frame that also results, is closer to Japan's medieval "In and around the capital" genre and Edo-period Rinpa school than the unified worlds seen in Western paintings.

Yuichi was a champion of Western art in the Meiji era who devoted his life to mastering its techniques. His paintings were outstanding in their ability to evoke a world of a sort never seen in Japan before. But at the same time, he was heir to an older way of seeing things that had survived the end of the Edo period. This is not a new observation,[5] but it is just as apparent in his still life work as elsewhere.

To actually produce these works, the first challenge Yuichi and his compatriots faced was procuring the necessary materials. Oil paint was in short supply in Meiji Japan, and brushes and canvases were not available in stores. However, Fontanesi brought a large supply of pigments and materials with him when he arrived to teach at the Technical Art School, and as appreciation for Western art rose, art supply stores dealing in both Japanese-made and imported wares opened their doors, finally allowing Japanese painters to freely obtain the materials they needed. In the January 10, 1878, edition of the *Yomiuri Shimbun*, the Itō Paint Store in Naka-chō, Fukagawa, advertised "oils and watercolors in every hue" as well as canvases, brushes, turpentine, varnish, brush washers, palettes, and busts, noting additionally that "other Japanese and imported supplies for painting in oils and watercolors arrive for sale daily."[6] The struggle to secure supplies had come to an end.

At around this time, in August 1877, Goseda Yoshimatsu won the Hōmon Prize at the First Domestic Industrial Exposition for his *Mount Fuji from the Abe River* (*Abekawa Fuji-zu*). The work itself is lost today, but some of the documentation Yoshimatsu produced as part of the entry process is still extant and describes how the work was painted, the materials used, and other details.[7] The account is difficult to understand today because of its now-outdated terminology for materials and chemicals, but according to modern art researcher Utada Shinsuke, Yoshimatsu began with a rough sketch in charcoal, finalized the composition in pencil, and then used a mixture of clay, judicious amounts of gum arabic, eggs, *shōchū* liquor, and vinegar to paint the undercoat. This was to prevent the outer layers of paint from peeling off. Whether Yoshimatsu always used an undercoat like this is uncertain, but Fontanesi had a similar practice which did indeed impart superior durability, as the condition of *Shinobazu Pond* shows.

With the undercoat complete, Yoshimatsu painted the scene from background to foreground, beginning with Mount Fuji in the upper part of the frame and ending with the Shizuoka City streets just before the viewer. (Few painters work this way today, but Yuichi is said to have painted in the same order as Yoshimatsu.) Once the painting was done, it was left to dry for sixty days and then given a final coat of varnish.[8]

Utada's account shows that Yoshimatsu, like Yuichi, had mastered and faithfully followed the traditional production process of the West. The same was probably true of all the painters of the Old School who studied at the Technical Art School. The result was that their works generally had a dark brown tone that saw them mocked as the "Resin school" (*yaniha*); the corresponding label applied to the New School was "Purple school" (*murasakiha*). Still, according to Utada—who has restored many paintings of the period—the old school did produce tougher painted surfaces.[9] Once Kuroda Seiki's new school had become the mainstream, dark colors fell out of favor, and some artists intentionally chose paints created to be less greasy. These trends can be connected to Japanese sensibilities in their own way, but the end result was that the work of these artists had problems with long-term durability.[10] Ultimately, the original techniques of oil painting imported from the West were preserved most faithfully in the Japan-made *wasei yuga* of the Old School.

III

As seen above, the first challenge the *wasei yuga* artists took up after mastering the traditional methods of the West was reproducing the visible world just as it was. When Takahashi Yuichi exhibited his still life paintings of kitchenware and other everyday items in his art school, the Tenkairō, visitors were startled by their realism: they were "just like looking at the real thing."[11] Later, after Fontanesi's arrival in Japan, Yuichi began representing three-dimensional space in his landscapes.[12] In *Distant View of Mount Kotohira* (p. 134), the flora foreground is rendered in superb close-up, but the sprawling space depicted extends to the distant blue sky. *Cityscape of Yamagata: Yamagata Kenchō-mae Street* (fig. 7), a painting based on a photograph, demonstrates skillful use of perspective. Still, like his still life works, these landscapes depicted only the visible world.

However, over the course of the 1880s a different trend emerged. "History paintings," depicting events that had taken place in the past rather than scenes viewed by the painter in the present, began to appear in great number. The history paintings on display at the Third Domestic Industrial Exposition in 1890 included Tsukahara Ritsuko's *Sei Shōnagon Visits Hatsuse*

Figure 7. Takahashi Yuichi, *Cityscape of Yamagata: Yamagata Kenchō-mae Street* (*Yamagata shigai-zu: Yamagata Kenchō-mae-dōri*), ca. 1881–1882. Yamagata Prefecture.

Figure 9. Honda Kinkichirō,
The Heavenly Maiden in the Legend of Hagoromo (Hagoromo tennyo), 1890.
Hyogo Prefectural Museum of Art.

Figure 8. Sakuma Bungo,
Wake no Kiyomaro Conveying the Gods' Message to the Empress (Wake no Kiyomaro, shinkyō o sō suru no zu), 1890. Sannomaru Shōzōkan.

Temple (Sei Shōnagon Hatsusedera ni mōzuru zu) and Sakuma Bungo's *Wake no Kiyomaro Conveying the Gods' Message to the Empress* (fig. 8), which won second and third prize respectively; Oka Seiichi's *Wife of Yamauchi Kazutoyo (Yamauchi Kazutoyo no tsuma),* which received an honorable mention); Honda Kinkichirō's *The Heavenly Maiden in the Legend of Hagoromo* (fig. 9); Goseda Hōryū's portrait *Saginuma Heikurō;* Indō Matate's *Enlistment of a Soldier in Ancient Times (Kodai ōbohei-zu);* and Jinnaka Itoko's *Murasaki Shikibu's Childhood (Murasaki Shikibu yōshō no zu).*[13]

The background to this development was a rising tide of interest in tradition, not only in the field of art but gradually becoming more apparent in every aspect of society. When the Technical Art School was forced to close just seven years after its opening, it was partly due to the financial pressures faced by the government, but the push to revive tradition—itself partly inspired by Ernest Fenollosa's reappraisal of Japanese art—was another contributing factor.

Viewed more broadly, the decision was just one of many actions taken at the time to preserve cultural treasures and create traditions. The policy of preserving Japan's "old customs" (*kyūkan*) began to be pursued in earnest after the Meiji Emperor's 1877 visit to Yamato (modern Nara Prefecture), the location of the old capital. The burial mounds of ancient emperors in Yamato were formally recognized, a Special National Treasure Research Bureau was established in 1888, and in 1890 Kashihara Shrine was constructed on the site in Yamato where the first Japanese emperor, Jinmu, was said to have been enthroned. The 1887 establishment of the Tokyo School of Fine Arts, which taught Japanese artistic technique exclusively, was also part of this trend.

This far-reaching return to tradition was neither mere reaction against the Westernization policies of the early Meiji period nor rooted in simple nostalgia. As historian Takagi Hiroshi rightly notes, these policies were based on the recognition by Iwakura Tomomi, Itō Hirobumi, and other key figures in the national government that "to form a constitutional state and become a first-class power in international society, the possession of a unique cultural 'tradition,' like the royalty of Russia, Austria, and England, was essential."[14] "Return to tradition" was not about "anti-Westernization" or "anti-modernity"; on the contrary, it was part of the modernization effort itself, one step in establishing a modern state that could stand alongside those of Western Europe. In that sense, it is connected to the same policy of Westernization that led to the construction of the European-style Rokumeikan in Tokyo to house and entertain foreign dignitaries. The completion in 1888 of the New Imperial Palace, with the help of countless Japanese artists, and the following year's promulgation of the Meiji Constitution and inaugural convention of the Imperial Diet were both the result of these efforts.

This being the case, it was only natural that interest in the nation's history should rise rapidly during this period. The subject of history was identified as particularly important in the *Guidelines for the Course of Study for Elementary Schools* issued by the Department of Education in May 1881, and from this time the course of study was said to have included only Japanese history.[15] The College of Letters of the Imperial University (today's Faculty of Letters at the University of Tokyo) had a History Division that taught Western history almost exclusively, but in 1889 a Japanese History Division was established as well.

One intellectual who anticipated the needs of the age with characteristic foresightedness and perceived the importance of history paintings was Okakura Tenshin. In the introduction to the inaugural issue of the art magazine *Flower of the Nation (Kokka)*, published in October 1889, Okakura observed that history paintings were "among the genres of painting whose development has been torpid in our nation"; however, he continued, "considering the future of painting ... history paintings should be promoted in accordance with the development of the idea of the national polity (*kokutai shisō*)."[16] As if in response, in December of that year craft historian Ōmori Ichū contributed a piece to *Garden of Art (Bijutsuen)* magazine entitled "The Necessity of History Paintings" (Rekishiga no hitsuyō) in which he demanded "Is not now the very time when history paintings are most needed?"[17] The numerous Western-style painters who tried their hand at history paintings for the Third Domestic Industrial Exhibition the following year, as described earlier, did so in the context of a strong contemporaneous trend towards exhibiting Japan's identity to the world in a visible form.

Naturally, Western-style painters had produced works demonstrating an interest in history before this. Rather than "history paintings" in the original (Western) usage of the word—paintings of a specific historical event—they might be more accurately called "historical personage paintings," depicting the people of the past in a form more comprehensible to modern viewers. Indō Matate's *Ancient Beauty* (fig. 10) is just one example of a Japanese painter stretching Western-style realism to encompass a

Figure 10. Indō Matate, *Ancient Beauty (Kodai bijin no zu)*, 1890. Tokyo University of the Arts.

broader "world" than what was currently visible. But the Third Domestic Industrial Exposition of 1890 is nevertheless noteworthy as an event at which the issue of themes in Western-style painting came to the fore. The lively response to and various debates sparked by Toyama Masakazu's lecture on "The Future of Japanese Painting," delivered to the second meeting of the Meiji Art Society while the Exposition was in progress, is eloquent testament to this fact.[18]

In the history of modern Japanese art, this period as a whole is sometimes viewed as a slow one for Western-style painting. But in the field of history paintings—not to mention landscape and genre painting, a topic for another essay—uncommonly rich results were achieved by the masters of *wasei yuga*.

Notes

1. Kume Kunitake, ed. *Britain*, trans. Graham Healey. Vol. 2 of *The Iwakura Embassy, 1871–1873: A True Account of the Ambassador Extraordinary and Plenipotentiary's Journal of Observation Through the United States of America and Europe* (Princeton: Princeton University Press, 2002).

2. For a detailed account of Honda's *Guide to Oil Painting* and its relationship to Takahashi Yuichi's technique, see Utada Shinsuke's *Aburae o kaibō suru: Shūfuku kara mita Nihon yōgashi* (Dissecting oil paintings: The history of Western painting in Japan seen through restoration; Tokyo: Nihon Hōsō Shuppan Kyōkai, 2002), pp. 106–122.

3. Barbara Bertozzi, "Antonio Fontanesi. La sua esperienza in Giappone" (Antonio Fontanesi: His experiences in Japan), p. 126. In *Antonio Fontanesi 1818–1882*, Torino: Umberto Allemandi, 1997. Published in conjunction with an exhibition of the same title curated by Rosanna Maggio Serra at the Galleria Civica d'Arte Moderna e Contemporanea.

4. The sole exception is Dutch painter Willem van Royen's *Birds and Flowers* painting, acquired in the 1720s at the request of the eighth shogun Yoshimune. The work was eventually gifted to Gohyaku Rakanji Temple and attracted much admiration as one of the temple's treasures.

5. For example, Sakakida Emiko's "Takahashi Yuichi ni tsuite no ni, san no mondai" (Two or three problems regarding Takahashi Yuichi) in *Bijutsushi*, vol. 115 (1983.11); Kōno Motoaki's "Takahashi Yuichi: Edo kaigashi no shiten kara" (Takahashi Yuichi from the perspective of Edo art history) in *Bakumatsu–Meiji no gakatachi: Bunmei kaika no hazama ni* (The painters of the Bakumatsu and Meiji periods: In the cracks of civilization and enlightenment; ed. Tsuji Nobuo; Tokyo: Pelican-sha, 1992); Kōno Motoaki's "Takahashi Yuichi: Kaizu" (Takahashi Yuichi's *Shells*) in *Kokka*, vol. 1334 (2006.12); and Furuta Ryō's *Kanō Hōgai–Takahashi Yuichi* (Kanō Hōgai and Takahashi Yuichi; Tokyo: Minerva Shobō, 2006).

6. Ishii Kendō, *Meiji jibutsu kigen* (Origin of things from the Meiji period; Tokyo: Nihon Hyōron-sha, 1969), p. 371.

7. Included in *Meiji bijutsu kiso shiryōshū* (Basic collection of materials on Meiji-period art; Tokyo: Tokyo National Research Institute for Cultural Properties, 1975).

8. Utada, *Yuga o kaibō suru* (see note 3), pp. 104–106.

9. Ibid, p. 85 and after.

10. Of course, durability is not necessarily lost whenever bright colors are used. Describing his experiences restoring Raphaël Collin's *Woman in White*, Utada observes that "Collin's oils are so firm that they feel like lacquer." Utada, *Yuga o kaibō suru* (see footnote 3), p. 122.

11. Andō Chūtarō, "Meiji shonen no yōga kenkyū" (Research on Western-style paintings of the early Meiji period), p. 57. In Aoki Shigeru, ed. *Meiji yōga shiryō: Kaisōhen* (Historical materials on Meiji-period Western paintings: Reminiscences; Tokyo: Chūokōron Bijutsu Shuppan, 1985).

12. Yuichi did not study at the Technical Art School himself, but he enrolled his son Genkichi there and is known to have met with Fontanesi often.

13. *Meiji bijutsukai hōkoku* (Meiji Art Society report), vols. 6–7.

14. Takagi Hiroshi, "1880-nendai, Yamato ni okeru bunkazai hogo" (Preservation of cultural assets in Yamato in the 1880s), p. 264. In *Kindai tennōsei no bunkashi-teki kenkyū* (Cultural-historical research on the modern imperial system; Tokyo: Azekura Shobō, 1997).

15. Included in Kitazawa Noriaki, ed. "Rekishi/kaiga nenpyō" (History/art chronology), in *Egakareta rekishi: Kindai Nihon bijutsu ni miru dentō to shinwa* (Painted history: Tradition and myth as seen in modern Japanese art), published in conjunction with an exhibition of the same title held in 1993 at the Hyogo Prefectural Museum of Modern Art and the Kanagawa Prefectural Museum of Modern Art.

16. *Kokka*, vol. 1 (1889.10), p. 2.

17. *Bijutsuen*, vol. 15 (1889.12.30), p. 30. (Quotation taken from p. 310 of reprinted edition: *Bijutsuen*, vol. 2. Tokyo: Yumani Shobō, 1991.)

18. For more on this point, see my "Meiji-ki rekishiga-ron josetsu" (An introduction to the history paintings of the Meiji period), in *Seiyō no me, Nihon no me* (Eyes of the West, eyes of Japan; Tokyo: Seido-sha, 2001).

Sentiment and Sensibility:
Beneath the Surface of *Wasei Yuga*

In the late 1970s, when I was a visiting professor at the newly opened Centre Georges Pompidou in Paris, I was assigned to teach a three-month series on Japanese art. The audience was largely made up of curators from the Centre and other museums in and around the city, including some friends with whom I would later organize an exhibition on *japonisme* at the Galeries nationales du Grand Palais and the National Museum of Western Art, Tokyo. All specialized in Western art, with very little connection to the art of Japan, modern or otherwise. The only Japanese painter they knew by name was Léonard Foujita, who achieved fame while resident in Europe. As a result, I began each lecture by reviewing the relevant historical background, introducing the participants to an artistic world that was, for them, completely uncharted territory. Their reactions to what I showed them exceeded my expectations in many intriguing ways.

For example, I had anticipated that artists like Kuroda Seiki, Okada Saburōsuke, and Umehara Ryūzaburō, who learned oil painting during extended stays in France, would interest my audience from a historical perspective, particularly regarding the question of French influence. But I was surprised by the audience's interest in and praise for the work of painters like Takahashi Yuichi, Aoki Shigeru, Kishida Ryūsei, and Koide Narashige. These artists received no direct instruction from French masters; in fact, with the exception of Koide, none of them travelled to Europe at all—and even Koide returned to Japan after just a few months, finding that Europe did not agree with him. As a result, despite their unsurpassed passion for

Western art and determination to learn its methods, these artists produced work with no visible traces of direct instruction from contemporary French painters, unlike those who actually studied overseas.

Aoki Shigeru made his name by participating in the exhibitions held by Kuroda's White Horse Society (Hakuba-kai), but the "impressionistic Academism" favored by the society's members was less influential on his art than turn-of-the-century Symbolists like Edward Burne-Jones, Pierre Puvis de Chavannes, and Gustave Moreau, whose phantasmagorical work was known to Aoki through art books and illustrations. Kishida Ryūsei was initially drawn to the fierce colors of Fauvism, but later retraced the history of Western art and devoted himself to the hard, minute realism of Albrecht Dürer. The dense expressiveness of the Northern Renaissance also aroused strong empathy in Koide Narashige, and he signaled as much by including an art book by Holbein in his *Mr. N's Family* (fig. 1), now recognized as an Important Cultural Property. As for Takahashi Yuichi, although not part of any particular tradition, he devoted himself body and soul to making the realistic expressive power of Western painting his own.

Because these Japanese painters were somewhat disconnected from the epochal changes that took place in the Paris-centric art world from the late nineteenth to the early twentieth century, they did not quite fit into the framework of modern art history as my audience understood it. Put an-

Figure 1. Koide Narashige, *Mr. N's Family* (*N. no kazoku*), 1919. Ōhara Museum of Art.

other way, because they did not—indeed, could not—learn from their French contemporaries, they were free to choose models for their work from art books and prints according to their own sensibilities rather than whatever movements happened to be active at the time.

The efforts of these painters to acquire Western painting techniques were thus supported by their sensibilities as Japanese artists. This combination gave rise to the phenomenon of *wasei yuga* or "Japan-made oil paintings" that I explored in the previous chapter. My audience at the Centre Pompidou was drawn to this body of work not just for its high degree of accomplishment and attractiveness but also by something else they sensed within it—something that could not be made to conform to the standards they were familiar with.

This is particularly apparent in the case of Takahashi Yuichi, an early pioneer and champion of Western painting in Japan. In his oft-quoted *Remarks from the Painting Bureau* (*Gagakukyoku tekigen*), Yuichi frankly describes his dissatisfaction with the "Japanese and Chinese painting methods" he initially learned and the passion he later poured into acquiring "the painting methods of the Occident." Supported by a clear will to technical mastery, that passion helped Yuichi overcome the lack of appropriate guides and models and become one of the most accomplished painters in the history of Western art in Japan. What he lacked in guidance and information he made up for with his essence as an artist: his way of seeing things, his approach to his subjects, his consciousness of space—in short, the *sensibility* behind his technique.

What set this sensibility slightly but decisively apart from that of a Western European artist? One aspect that is readily visible in Yuichi's art, alongside the vivid, almost palpable depiction of textural details of his subjects, is the extremely limited spaces in which those subjects are placed. In the classical still-life paintings of the West like seventeenth-century Dutch "banquet pieces" and *vanitas* paintings, a variety of objects are arranged on a surface like a table that extends towards the horizon, forming a clear three-dimensional space. In Yuichi's still-life paintings, on the other hand, the spaces inhabited by subjects tend to be surprisingly shallow, or even have no depth to speak of at all.

In *Tofu* (p. 119), textures are depicted with marvelous skill: the raw tofu looks genuinely cold to the touch, the oiliness of the fried tofu is almost palpable, and even the scars left by the knife on the chopping board are faithfully recreated. The board itself, however, is depicted from a slightly raised angle, and as a result it extends further to the left and right than it does away from the viewer toward the rear of the tableau. In the same way, Yuichi's *Cod and Plum Blossoms* (fig. 2) conveys the damp surface of the cod, the roughness of the rope, and the fine details of the flowers with powerful realism, but because the surface on which the bowl is placed is

Figure 2.
Takahashi Yuichi,
*Cod and Plum
Blossoms*
(*Tara baika*), 1877.
Kotohiragū Shrine.

Figure 3.
Takahashi Yuichi,
Sea Bream (Tai), 1879.
Kotohiragū Shrine.
(See plate 16)

viewed from above, there is almost no sense of depth. As for the well-known *Salmon* (p. 91), currently in the collection of the Tokyo University of the Arts, the rear of the tableau is completely closed off, resulting in a visible space that is only as deep as the solid-looking salmon itself plus the slight gap implied by its shadow.

Remove all the tableware and fruit from a Dutch still life and the depth of space implied by the table would still exist. Remove the motifs from *Cod with Plum Blossoms* or *Salmon*, though, and no hint of depth would remain. The same can be said of *Sea Bream* (fig. 3), which shows prawns, fish, and daikon arranged around a formidable central sea bream in a depiction of an abundant festival-time feast, and the superb *Reader and Notebook* (p. 120), in which the diversity of motifs and vivid sense of color leaves a deep impression. In *Reader and Notebook* in particular, the spatial relationship between the objects on the desk—the elementary school reader, battledore, ball, paper, and pencil—and the half-seen lantern and notebook hanging at the top of the frame is somewhat unclear. Rather than constructing a "container" of three-dimensional space for all the objects to reside in together, Yuichi simply recreated the physical presence of each from as close a viewpoint as possible.

Depicting subjects in detail from close range and framing compositions from an elevated angle both tend to flatten the tableau rather than creating a space with depth. This flattening is particularly apparent in Yuichi's still lifes, but it is not unique to his work: it is also an important characteristic in traditional Japanese painting. For example, consider the *tagasode* (literally "Whose sleeves?") genre of paintings popular during the Edo period. While technically interior still lifes, depicting women's kimonos on a rack, these paintings establish no three-dimensional space. They do, however, intricately depict the patterns on the kimonos themselves down to the finest detail. And, as discussed in previous chapters, the "In and around the capital" genre of cityscapes featured flattened compositions due to their elevated overall viewpoint. "Champion of the Western art world" though Yuichi was, he nevertheless inherited the traditional sensitivities of Japanese artists of the Edo period and after—although he might not have been conscious of this himself.

In landscapes, the extension of space is an important theme in itself.

But even when Yuichi rose to the challenge of representing space receding into the depths of the tableau, he made use of close-up viewpoints, too. For example, in his largest, boldest painting, *Distant View of Mount Kotohira* (fig. 4), the verdant mountain stands calmly at the center of the background, silhouetted by the bright blue sky, but the riot of grasses and flowers in the foreground is depicted in exquisite detail. The foreground flora are shown in extreme close-up in *Distant View of Asakusa* (*Asakusa tenbō*), too, all but dominating the painting. In *Shinobazu Pond* (fig. 5), the branches of the willows swaying in the wind at the top of the frame are so large they seem to hang right before the viewer.

Experiments in juxtaposing a foreground motif in extreme close-up with a distant background date back to the second half of eighteenth century, as seen in Akita *Ranga* school standard-bearer Odano Naotake's own *Shinobazu Pond* (fig. 6), now an Important Cultural Property. Similarly, the compositional technique of allowing the edge of the frame to cut off the foreground motif for stronger contrast can be seen in *Pine Tree and Exotic Bird* (fig. 7) by Satake Shozan, another Akita *Ranga* painter. Hiroshige was also fond of the technique, as is particularly apparent in "Horikiri Iris Garden" (Horikiri no hanashōbu), "Plum Estate, Kameido" (fig. 8), and "Ushimachi, Takanawa" (Takanawa Ushimachi) in his *One Hundred Famous Views of Edo*.

Figure 4. Takahashi Yuichi, *Distant View of Mount Kotohira* (*Kotohirayama Enbō*), 1881. Kotohiragū Shrine.

Figure 5. Takahashi Yuichi, *Shinobazu Pond* (*Shinobazu no ike*), ca. 1880. Aichi Prefectural Museum of Art.

Figure 6. Odano Naotake, *Shinobazu Pond* (*Shinobazu no ike*), 1770s. Akita Museum of Modern Art.

Figure 7. Satake Shozan, *Pine Tree and Exotic Bird* (*Matsu ni karatori*), eighteenth century. Private collection.

In any case, given the startlement of French painters like Degas and Van Gogh at the eccentric compositions of Japanese art when *japonisme* was at its height, it seems fair to say that this combination of nearness and distance in Yuichi's landscapes was a Japanese characteristic (fig. 9). We might also note that these views of Asakusa and Shinobazu Pond—not to mention other subjects of Yuichi's, like Mount Fuji, Enoshima, and Futamigaura—also hint at the "pictures of famous places" (*meisho-e*) genre as it was practiced in the Edo period. A certain Japanese sensibility which does not fit neatly into the framework of Western art's development during this period is one major factor in the anti-contemporary and irresistible appeal of Takahashi Yuichi's oeuvre.

This uniquely Japanese sensibility left its mark on all *wasei yuga* to some extent. For example, the nude as a genre was imported from the West, but while Kishida Ryūsei aimed to depict his reclining subjects with a sense of solidity, his placement of the background behind them parallel to the frame betrays a certain tendency toward flatness of overall composition. Koide Narashige's *Nude on Bed* (*Nude A*) (*Shina shindai no rafu [Ē no rajo]*), in which the bed is viewed from above, also evokes this Japanese sensibility. Mitsutani Kunishirō traveled to France and studied the techniques of Western Academism with Jean-Paul Laurens, but proved that the same sensibility still lived within him later in life by returning to an extremely Japanese style of expression for *Scarlet Rug* (fig. 10).

In this respect, the road traveled by Ryūsei, whose passion for realism invites comparison to Takahashi Yuichi, is of great interest. In his early

Figure 8. Utagawa Hiroshige, "Plum Estate, Kameido" (Kameido Ume-yashiki) from *One Hundred Famous Views of Edo* (*Meisho Edo hyakkei*), 1857. National Diet Library. (See plate 17)

Figure 9. Vincent van Gogh, *Flowering Plum Orchard (after Hiroshige)* (*Bloeiende pruimen-boomgaard [naar Hiroshige]*), 1887. Van Gogh Museum, Amsterdam (Vincent van Gogh Foundation). (See plate 18)

Figure 10. Mitsutani Kunishirō,
Scarlet Rug (*Himōsen*), 1932.
Ōhara Museum of Art.

Figure 11. Yorozu Tetsugorō,
Self-Portrait with Clouds
(*Kumo no aru jigazō*), 1912.
Ōhara Museum of Art.

Figure 12. Sekine
Shōji, *Sorrow of
Faith* (*Shinkō no
kanashimi*), 1918.
Ōhara Museum
of Art.

works, he dallied with fierce colors recalling Van Gough and the Fauvists, as well as the pleinairism of the White Horse Society, but he later moved towards the gloomy, meticulous style of Dürer. Tracing the history of Western art backwards puts him at odds with his times, but the Japanese sensibility identified above is revealed most clearly at the pinnacle of his artistic achievement: his many portraits of his daughter Reiko. In these works, Reiko herself is depicted with exquisite realism and overwhelming solidity and presence, but her surroundings are a dark space with a closed-off background. Kishida lived only to the age of 38, but his attraction to the tastes of Edo in his later years is highly suggestive.

Alongside these distinctively Japanese approaches to subjects and spatial composition, the lineage of what we might call "paintings of sentiment" is worth considering. Beginning with Aoki Shigeru and transmitted to Kumagai Morikazu, Yorozu Tetsugorō, and Sekine Shōji, this approach depicts a fiercely dense, sometimes phantasmagorical world utterly unlike the brightly shining real world outdoors. The self-assertion visible in Aoki's *Face of a Man* (*Otoko no kao*) and Yorozu's *Self-portrait with Clouds* (fig. 11); the vehement, wordless lament of Kumagai's *The Day My Son Yō Died* (*Yō no shinda hi*); the unsettling fantasy of Sekine's *Sorrow of Faith* (fig. 12), an Important Cultural Property—it is precisely the weight of the sentiment pent up within these works that gives them their powerful appeal.

Even the most distinctively Japanese *wasei yuga* obviously used techniques derived ultimately from the oil paintings of Western Europe. Nevertheless, artists who absorbed these techniques did not necessarily abandon their unique Japanese sensibility. On the contrary: It was precisely this sensibility, combined with their fierce individuality, that allowed these artists to create a unique world of form and expression the likes of which the West had never seen.

Japan and the West in the Art of Takeuchi Seihō

Takeuchi Seihō was a man of keen eye, and this eye served him over the course of his life as an artist. He spent his childhood engrossed in sketching the animals, birds, and flowers around him; as a teacher, he insisted that his pupils see subjects through their own eyes rather than borrowing the views of others. He understood the skill of drawing from life, however an artist may develop it, is the foundation for all forms of pictorial expression.

The eye with which Seihō approached his own drawing from life is readily apparent in the records of and interviews relating to his trip to Europe in 1900–1901 to see the Exposition universelle in Paris and the art galleries of the continent's chief cities. Departing Kōbe aboard the NYK ship the *Wakasa Maru* on August 1, 1900, Seihō arrived in Marseille on September 17. Seihō spent the seven-week voyage studying the exotic scenes full of unfamiliar people and things that unfolded before his eyes, and the special attention he paid to the distinctive colors of each location speaks to his eye as a painter. In an interview conducted after Seihō's return by Kuroda Tengai for the *Kyoto Hinode Shimbun*, Seihō says:

> So, first we go to Hong Kong, and the atmosphere changes: the rickshaw's wheels are painted white and green, their canopies are white, from the shape of the chairs to the look of the sails on ships, the hulls of the ships are tinted all kinds of colors, and on the prow there are large eyeballs, the whole thing's colored like a dragon with *ungen* (gradated) tones, and the overall color scheme is typically

Chinese. … You get the sense that these are what you might call the colors of that country.

When we come to the tropics, the colors are tropical: the trees are greener, the houses are painted with thin whitish colors, the people are very black, and what they wear around their waist is often striped, with red colors used a lot, which becomes a sort of unique characteristic. And the vacantly standing camels, the deserts that go on for thousands of miles, the reflection of the evening sun in the burnt-out mountains, the endless blue sea … There are places that would make a good painting, and I think that each color scheme naturally represents that country's unique characteristics.

The key point is that each region, from Egypt or Europe, has its own color scheme and material culture. Without examining the "atmosphere and characteristics" of other countries, Seihō continues, "you can't master those of Japan either." In order to create the new Japanese painting, the methods of Western art cannot be rejected in their entirety, but neither should they be accepted just as they are. The unique characteristics of Western painting must first be studied exhaustively, after which the painter, Seihō explains, should adopt only what is required by the realities of Japan. The reception of ideas should be purposeful and independent.

For example, oil painting techniques that were highly effective at recreating reality were perfected quite early in the West through close observation of light and color, but it would not do to apply those techniques unconditionally in Japan. This, Seihō says, is because "the air in the West is thick, so the contrast between near and far is extremely noticeable, but returning to Japan you find the air transparent and thin; by making sure the quality of the light and so on is right for Japan, I hope to create the perfect picture." Throughout the interview Seihō exhibits an extremely self-aware attitude towards adopting the things of the West. In fact, upon his return from Europe he even changed the characters used to write "Seihō"—the name he received from his teacher Kōno Bairei—to incorporate the character for "West."

Seihō was open to many influences. In his 1892 painting *Cat and Kittens Lazing in the Sun* (*Byōji fuken*), the posture and fur of the cats are inherited from the Maruyama school, but the grass and flowers are of the Shijō and the rocks of the Kanō school. As a result, the painting was mockingly described as a work of the "*Nue* school," a reference to a chimera-like hybrid monster of Japanese legend. This well-known episode demonstrates the universal assumption at the time that an aspiring painter would find a teacher and learn to paint in their school alone.

It was true that entering the tutelage of a master and studying the techniques illustrated in the examples they assigned was the normal route to becoming an artist of good standing in that period. Seihō, too, was thoroughly trained in the Maruyama–Shijō school of painting under Bairei. He was even appointed senior craftsman (*kōgeichō*) ahead of his seniors at the school in recognition of his outstanding talent. But Seihō never restricted himself to that tradition alone. He studied a range of painting techniques, and, even as his fellow students occupied themselves almost exclusively with model paintings in the school, went out into the streets to draw from life. In other words, he showed no sign of any intention to inherit and protect the traditions of any school as such; instead, he considered it natural to adopt, without prejudice, whatever would be useful for his creative expression.

Seihō's attitude towards Western art was no different. Excluding travel time to and from Europe, his tour of the continent lasted just four months, but in those four months he visited eight different countries. As well as seeing the Exposition universelle, he found time to visit Europe's great museums and consider how what was superior in the art of the West could be adopted to make up for what Japanese painting lacked. Seihō called the French paintings at the Exposition refined and "urbane"; the German works "unpolished," with dense, dark color schemes; and the English works "almost transparent in their clarity"—all accurate characterizations. Seihō further admired the way each country's art "created a form" based on thorough preparation and argued that this approach must be brought into the world of Japanese painting too.

While in France, Seihō also visited the professor of art Jean-Léon Gérôme and quizzed him on the trials of recreating a subject; later, at an art school in Dresden, he requested (and was granted) special permission to observe nude life drawing, the basis for depictions of the human form.

These encounters brought Seihō into contact with the roots of realism, and he concluded as a result that to improve Japanese painting it would be necessary to follow the example set by the West and study posture and form directly from life. Regarding the human form in particular, he noted, knowledge of anatomy would be an unavoidable necessity.

Despite his punishing schedule, Seihō did not forget to seize what opportunities he could to sketch the sights and animals of the foreign lands he passed through. He himself later admitted to extending his stay in Antwerp for three whole weeks longer than originally planned in order to visit the zoo and sketch the lions in their cage. Furthermore, recognizing that he would not be able to see everything in the limited time he had, Seihō bought photographic references and picture postcards in vast quantities to supplement his own eye. He used these materials to fuel his creative activities after returning home, even grappling with the techniques of oil painting: his *Suez Landscape* (fig. 1), painted in oils and exhibited at the First Kansai Art Exhibition immediately after his return, was a triumph for the *Nue* school. (Incidentally, this work—invaluable as the only surviving oil painting by Seihō—went missing after the exhibition and was not rediscovered until 2014.)

Seihō's visit to Europe was a major turning point in his life as a painter. It made his unfailing eye for the real world even sharper, helped him learn specific Western techniques like the use of light and shade for expressing

Figure 1.
Takeuchi Seihō,
Suez Landscape
(*Suezu keshiki*), 1901.
Umi-Mori Art Museum.

that world in the frame, and inspired him to experiment further with adopting these techniques in his own work. But none of this meant that Seihō viewed art as a matter of simply recreating a subject exactly as it appeared. In his view, the techniques of realism were only the foundation: the task of art was to transcend mere recreation of the natural world and express something that appealed directly to the human heart and evoked emotion within it.

For example, in the context of adopting Western realism into Japanese ink wash painting, Seihō argued that the movement between dark and light in the tone of the ink must be "more exquisite than in the sketches 'over there'" (using a common term for the West at the time). Similarly, the "unique brushwork" of Japanese painting made development of "sensitivity and taste" an absolute necessity.

Going further, despite the differing histories of Japanese and Western painting, Seihō held that insofar as they represented "subtle truths of the heart" on a foundation of "realism," they were identical. The underlying theme of Seihō's terminology—"exquisite," "taste and sensitivity," "subtle truths of the heart"—is what might be called *poetic sentiment*, appealing directly to the emotions. Or, to borrow a Japanese word used often at the time, *shai* ("representation of spirit") as opposed to *shajitsu* ("representation of substance").

In a report he made to the Kyoto Art Association after his return from Europe, Seihō attributed the following thoughts on *shai* to an American painter he happened to meet:

Western paintings are like reflections in a mirror: they lack imagination, amounting to nothing more than seeing forms as they are. Outside this, they offer no interest. The emphasis in Japanese painting on the representation of spirit is something I admire. If art is not poetic, it cannot be sublime. It is only when art exhibits a kind of transcendental accomplishment that it begins to be valuable.

Seihō concurs, saying, "This argument captures my thinking on this matter precisely."

As an example of this kind of thinking in action, consider *Spring Light in*

Figure 3. Takeuchi Seihō,
Historic Spot of Rome
(*Rōma no zu*), 1903.
Umi-Mori Art Museum.

Holland/Autumn Colors in Italy (fig. 2), which Seihō exhibited at the Exhibition of New and Antique Art the year after his return from Europe. This pair of six-panel folding screens shows an ancient Italian ruin on the left and one of the Netherlands' famous windmills on the right. Both motifs and their sprawling, unspoiled settings are surely based on Seihō's records from Europe and the photographic references he brought home with him, but neither screen depicts a scene he actually saw. Seihō's trip through Europe lasted from summer through winter—he had never seen the Netherlands in spring, and nor did he know Italy in autumn, since he visited Venice and Rome only toward the end of his journey in December. The compositional contrast of "spring light" with "autumn colors" on a pair of folding screens is the traditional Japanese sensitivity to the passage of seasons at work.

Similar observations could be made about *Historic Spot of Rome* (fig. 3),

Figure 2. Takeuchi Seihō,
*Spring Light in Holland/
Autumn Colors in Italy*
(*Oranda shunkō/Itaria
shūshoku*), 1902.

exhibited at the Fifth Domestic Industrial Exhibition in 1903. This work, too, is a pair of landscape paintings on six-panel folding screens, this time featuring two ancient ruins: the Temple of Minerva Medica on the left, and the Aqua Claudia on the right.

Paintings of ruins enjoyed a wave of popularity in Europe starting around the middle of the eighteenth century. Many artists made the pilgrimage to the ruins of ancient Rome to rue its lost glory and paint melancholy meditations on its rise and fall. Foremost among them was the French painter Hubert Robert, who even earned the nickname "Robert of the Ruins." Parallel to this trend, collections of prints and photographs were published which provided an archaeological view of ancient ruins. Both the Temple of Minerva Medica and the Aqua Claudia were popular for this sort of "sightseeing," and there was no shortage of artistic depictions of these sites. Whether Seihō saw the ruins himself is uncertain, but both can be found in the photographic references he brought back to Japan with him, and it seems likely that these were the basis for this work. In any case, however, his approach to their depiction was highly idiosyncratic.

In Western paintings of ruins, whatever crumbling structures or overgrown stones are visible are usually placed in the central foreground to help them stand out. Photographs are composed in the same way. But Seihō pushes the ruins to the rear of his paintings, replacing them in the foreground with rows of trees and even a woman leading goats. The ruins are clearly recognizable, of course, but they seem less "theme" than "background." It would be more accurate to describe the resultant tableaus as landscapes suffused with sentiment for ruins than paintings of ruins as such.

This, in turn, goes back to the unique aesthetic consciousness cultivated by the Japanese over centuries of intimate coexistence with nature and its unhurried yet constant change. Time flows without ceasing, and the turn of the seasons never slows. Both the festive beauty of the cherry blossoms in spring and the vivid glow of the autumn leaves vanish before long. And as nature changes, so too does the beauty within it. In Japan, this produced an "aesthetics of change," which saw beauty as fleeting, mutable, and therefore all the more precious and worthy of pining over.

Ruins, in their own way, are another example of this slow but inexorable passing away. Seihō's goal was not simply to depict how these relics of ancient times looked today, like Western painters. Rather, he sought to arouse an emotional response in the viewer by showing the ruins fading slowly alongside the changes of nature, to create what he referred to as a "transcendental accomplishment"—in other words, poetic sentiment itself. It is when we recognize this that we can recognize that Seihō, the man of keen eye, was also a man of unsurpassed sentiment and an heir to the traditional sensibilities of Japan.

III

Roots of the Japanese
Aesthetic Consciousness

Word and Image

Among the "poems of celebration" in the tenth-century *Kokin wakashū* anthology is the following poem by the Buddhist priest Sosei:

yorozuyo o	forever do I long
matsu ni zo kimi o	my lord, to dwell
iwaitsuru	beneath the pine
chitose no kage ni	rejoicing in its shelter
suman to omoeba	for a thousand years

The poem congratulates its recipient on his longevity by evoking the pine, said to live thousands or even tens of thousands of years, and expresses warm wishes for many more. Its headnote reads "Composed for the celebration of Yoshimine no Tsunenari's fortieth birthday on behalf of his daughter," indicating that the "lord" of the poem is Tsunenari himself.

When this poem was composed, it was customary for landmark birthdays like the fortieth and seventieth to be celebrated with gifts of poetry from friends and family. Guests lacking in poetic skill presumably engaged the services of a professional like Sosei or Ki no Tsurayuki instead.

Here, for example, is one of Tsurayuki's "poems of celebration" in the *Kokin wakashū*:

haru kureba	when spring comes
yado ni mazu saku	the first to flower in my yard

ume no hana	are the blossoms of the plum
kimi ga chitose no	which seem to me a garland
kazashi to zo miru	for your thousand years, my lord

According to its headnote, this poem was "written on the folding screen behind Prince Motoyasu at his seventieth birthday celebration." The specific phrasing used implies that a folding screen painted with a tableau of early spring plum blossoms stood behind the guest of honor at this celebratory feast, and Tsurayuki wrote his poem inspired by that painting. Whether written directly on the painting or on a separate piece of paper that was later pasted on, the beauty of the characters in Tsurayuki's flowing hand no doubt became another sight for the guests to admire.

Neither of these screens survives today, but the tradition of combining pictures, words (poetry), and calligraphy into a unified artistic world remained vibrant in Japan for centuries, inspiring countless masterpieces.

The eighteenth-century Pine and Wisteria *Maki-e* Lacquered Comb Box is one example. An ornamental design combining pine trees and wisteria executed in slightly raised gold *maki-e* covers the entire lid of the box, and the poem by Sosei quoted above is superimposed on this in silver *hyōmon* (inlaid strips of metal). The background design and the poem are connected by the auspicious motif of the pine tree; presumably, the box was made to congratulate someone on some now-forgotten achievement. What is most

Anonymous, Pine and Wisteria
Maki-e Lacquered Comb Box
(Matsu-fuji maki-e kushibako),
Mid-Edo period.

intriguing, however, is the way the poem is written. The individual *kana* characters are highly stylized, with unusually extended lines that visually echo the trailing wisteria in the background. In other words, the characters are not just symbols: they also play a role as plastic elements in the tableau.

The Japanese have long been fond of *moji-e* or "character-pictures," in which Chinese *kanji* or Japanese *kana* characters are used to draw a picture. Children still draw the *henohenomoheji* face and the *hemamushi nyūdō* today, and Japanese artists, without losing that playful spirit, raised *moji-e* to a form of expression of extreme refinement and elegance.

The "Hatsune" *Maki-e* Box (p. 70), said to have formed part of the trousseau of third Tokugawa shogun Iemitsu's daughter, is a good example of this. As discussed in the first section of this book, the box's lid is decorated with a sprawling garden in which stands a prominent pine tree. The tree is drawn using characters which combine with other characters hidden in the tableau to form part of the poem that Akashi sends to her daughter in the "Hatsune" ("The Warbler's First Song") chapter of the *Tale of Genji*:

toshitsuki o	let she who has waited
matsu ni hikarete	months and years, drawn
furu hito ni	always to the pine
kyō uguisu no	hear this day the warbler's
hatsune kikaseyo	first spring song

Taken together, the characters constitute a hint that allows us to recognize the picture on the lid as a scene from *The Tale of Genji*.

Narrow Path with Ivy, a painted screen by Tawaraya Sōtatsu (or at least his studio) and today recognized as an Important Cultural Property, is another example of writing used pictorially. *The Tales of Ise*, a loose narrative in prose and poetry dating to the early Heian period, supplies both the scene depicted and the poem written directly on the picture. Not only does the poem invite the viewer into the long-ago world described by Heian literature, the calligraphy echoes the rhythm of the ivy trailing into the frame from above, decorating the scene just as the ivy leaves do. The result is a spectacular duet of word and picture.

Words and pictures have always been highly compatible in Japan. In the

West, they were considered two entirely separate worlds. Even the tools used were different: pictures were painted with a soft brush, and text written with a hard stylus. In Japan, however, the same brush was used for both, reinforcing the sense of fellowship between them. The same is true of China, of course, where since ancient times "painting and calligraphy" (*shūhuà*) was considered a single genre. And, of course, by virtue of their origin, Chinese characters are highly representative, making them better suited to mingling with the world of pictures. The further simplification of Chinese characters into the abstract shapes of the *kana* syllabary in Japan also greatly expanded the possibilities for plastic expression through writing.

In the "Umegae" ("The Plum Tree Branch") chapter of the *Tale of Genji*, the author observes that the courtiers and nobles of the time were fond of "reed writing" (*ashide*), a game rich in artistry whose players competed to conceal text in paintings of waterside scenes. It is no coincidence that the popularity of "*ashide* pictures" coincided with the emergence of the *kana* syllabary. The tradition which developed from this saw art and literature—pictures and words—as bound firmly together into a single unit, an idea which gave birth to many highly refined forms of artistic expression.

Although text was often accompanied by ornamental figures or illustrations in the West, too, the separation of text and pictures on the page remained fundamental. Even in the illuminated manuscripts of the medieval period, pictures were usually drawn as decorations in the borders, or in

Tawaraya Sōtatsu (or his studio), *Narrow Path with Ivy* (*Tsuta no hosomichi byōbu*), seventeenth century. Shōkokuji Jōtenkaku Museum.

specific areas set aside for that purpose. With the exception of particularly elaborate illustrated capitals, they did not mingle with the text itself. The invention of the printing press in the fifteenth century reinforced the separation between text and image due to technical differences: movable type was used for text, and copperplate or other printing techniques for images. As lithographic technology became more sophisticated, works combining words and pictures—like the posters of Toulouse-Lautrec—did begin to appear, but this did not happen until the late nineteenth century.

In any case, countries that used the alphabet have no parallel to the Japanese tradition of drawing pictures with text—and meaningful, literary text, at that—that produced works like the "Hatsune" Box. The first experiment in arranging the words of poems to form pictures in the West is said to have been Apollinaire's *Calligrammes*, making this a twentieth-century phenomenon. Consider "It's Raining" (Il pleut), which begins with the line:

Il pleut des voix de femmes comme si elles étaient mortes même dans le souvenir
It's raining the voices of women as if they were dead even in memory

The poem invokes a lost love with the same sense of agonizing regret as "Mirabeau Bridge" (Le Pont Mirabeau), another well-known work by Apollinaire, but is distinguished by the fact that each of its rather long phrases is written in a single line across the page from upper left to lower right, like diagonally falling rain.

Apollinaire wrote many "calligrams" of this sort: one about a fountain, shaped like a spray of water; one about a heart, with lines arranged into the appropriate shape. The results are barely more than simple games, but in the absence of a *moji-e* tradition in the West they were received as bold, avant-garde gestures.

Startling as they were, however, Apollinaire's experiments with calligrams inspired no imitators, and poetry soon returned to the world of unaccompanied text. This was no doubt partly because arrangements of movable type were simply not suitable for pictorial expression. It is worth noting that in Apollinaire's original manuscript of "It's Raining," each line was written in cursive; by comparison, the distinct characters of the printed version can hardly be called "flowing."

Movable type was not unknown in Japan, even as early as the Edo period. The first shogun, Tokugawa Ieyasu, had types cast that still survive, as do the books they were used to produce, known as "Suruga editions" (*Suruga-ban*) after the location of the printing press. Ultimately, though, the new European technology simply did not find a place in Japan. Woodblock printing was used for everything, from ukiyo-e to illustrated books like *kibyōshi*. This surely represented, above all, a reluctance to separate pictures from text. This Japanese sensibility, in which words and pictures are seen as a single unit, remains alive today; consider, for example, *Wandering Away from Home* (*Ryūri-shō*), a work based on the poetry of Yoshii Isamu that might be called Munakata Shikō's masterpiece, or his prints inspired by the poetry of Tanizaki Jun'ichirō (*Utauta hanga-saku*). The colorful and free use of lettering in Japanese manga, too, is surely part of the reason for their popularity around the world today, and one might even argue that the smiling faces and other emoji used by young people in e-mails are another continuation of this thousand-year tradition.

(2004)

Chinese Characters and the Japanese Language

In *Ceci n'est pas une pipe*, his book about the work of Magritte, Michel Foucault identifies the separation between plastic representation and linguistic reference as the primary principle of Western painting from the fifteenth through to the twentieth century. As a result, he says, "these two systems could neither intersect nor blend together." Put more dramatically, pictures and text constituted completely separate worlds. But this observation is restricted to the Western European cultural sphere; in the East, it does not hold. In China just as in Japan, words and pictures were considered highly compatible, as the existence of a single genre known as *shūhuà* (literally "calligraphy and painting") suggests, intersecting and blending together as a matter of course.

As early as the second half of the nineteenth century, when *japonisme* saw vast quantities of Japanese artworks and crafts shipped to its West, people were noticing this difference with surprise. Indeed, Louis Gonse, whose 1883 *L'Art japonais* was the first book-length treatment of its subject in the West, openly admired the fact that the Japanese wrote and painted with the same brush; like the other critics who contributed to the lavish magazine *Le Japon artistique*, he considered the results superb. When Van Gogh, another artist strongly drawn to Japanese ukiyo-e, copied "Plum Estate, Kameido" (p. 136) from Hiroshige's *One Hundred Famous Views of Edo*, he added some Japanese writing to the left and right of the scene that was not only not in the original but actually had nothing to do with Hiroshige's work at all. Presumably he felt that this addition would make his work seem more "Japan-like."

The affinity between word and image that Western audiences found so fresh and striking was indeed partly rooted in the use of a shared brush. At the same time, though, it was partly made possible by the unique characteristics of the Japanese writing system itself. The Japanese characters—originally from China, of course—that Van Gogh struggled so to copy out are far more complex and diverse, and therefore more richly plastic, than the letters of the alphabet. You might say that *kanji*—the Japanese word for Chinese characters, especially those used to write Japanese—are more compatible with pictures by their very nature.

The diversity of *kanji* is a major cause of the complexity often bemoaned by foreign students of the Japanese language. In English, the same twenty-six letters are sufficient for everything from shopping lists to Shakespeare, but the thousands of *kanji* that must be learned for Japanese represent a more formidable task.

This argument has been made repeatedly even in Japan. Beginning in the Meiji period (1868–1912) but particularly in the Taisho period that followed (1912–1926), reformers insisted that the effort and time required to learn *kanji* was so great that they should be abandoned and replaced with a simple romanized orthography. Their efforts were ultimately unsuccessful, but one can draw a line from those arguments to the *kanji* restriction policies of the postwar period, which sought to standardize and limit the characters in common use.

However, any side-by-side comparison of *kanji* and the Roman alphabet contains within it a major error. The alphabet is phonetic, representing sound only, but *kanji* are also ideographic, representing meaning. A single *kanji*, like 山 (mountain) or 河 (river), can convey both the sound and meaning of an entire word, but a single letter cannot. As symbols representing sound alone, letters only convey meaning when combined appropriately: *mountain, river*.

In other words, *kanji* correspond not to letters but to words. If a comparison is to be made, they should be compared to the English lexicon. Just as non-native speakers have difficulty learning the individual shape and meaning of each *kanji*, learners of English face about the same difficulty learning the shape (spelling) and meaning of words. In terms of sheer number, the size of the English lexicon is far more reminiscent of the number of *kanji*. The works of Shakespeare are said to contain 15,200 distinct words. Shakespeare might be an atypical example, but at least two or three thousand words would surely be necessary to understand and use English normally. The number of *kanji* used in everyday contexts is roughly the same.

Shirakawa Shizuka's examination of the Chinese classics found just 1,355 distinct characters in the *Analects* of Confucius. Even the *Classic of Poetry* uses just 2,839. A student who learns a few thousand Chinese characters can read those two works. In purely numerical terms, compared to the *Analects*, reading Shakespeare calls for ten times as much study.

Naturally, having both phonetic and ideographic function does make *kanji* inconvenient at times. Even when the intention is to use them for solely phonetic purposes, meaning is prone to leak in.

Consider *Beikoku*, a Japanese word for America. Although the word is written with characters that literally mean "rice country" (米国), this does not mean that America is considered a major source or producer of rice. The character for "rice" was simply adopted from another, phonetic way to write *America*: 亜米利加. If this sort of background information is unknown, however, grave misunderstandings can arise.

For instance, in China, the corresponding word for *America* is *Meiguo*, literally written "beautiful country" (美国). The first time I visited Hong Kong, I was very confused when I saw graffiti reading "Down With the Beautiful Country!" on a wall. I did not realize until someone explained it to me later that the literal meaning "beautiful country" was irrelevant.

In cases like this, a non-ideographic writing system like an alphabet would be a convenient thing to have. Within a Chinese character–using culture that lacks a purely phonetic system, even the hated America becomes the "beautiful country."

In Japan, however, not only were Chinese characters successfully adopted and mastered as *kanji*, a phonetic writing system capable of standing shoulder-to-shoulder with the alphabet was also born: the *kana* characters. Writing in Japan today mixes *kanji* and *kana* as a matter of course, but I doubt there is any other orthography that mixes two very different systems so naturally.

In fact, during the reception of Chinese characters, Japan was the home of another innovation. The characters were accepted as they were, but the sounds of a completely different language—*Yamato-kotoba*, the Japanese language of the time—were added to them. These are known as *kun* ("interpretive") readings of the characters, as opposed to the *on* ("phonetic") readings corresponding to the original Chinese pronunciation—a distinction still in use today. *Kun* readings made it easier for Chinese characters to take root in Japanese soil and are another example of the tendency in Japan's national character to proactively adopt new things while preserving the old.

Ki no Tsurayuki's so-called *"Kana* preface" to the *Kokin wakashū* begins, as is well known, with the statement "Japanese poetry has the human heart as its seed and grows into myriad leaves of words." Tsurayuki's use of the term "Japanese poetry" (*Yamato-uta*) presumably implies an opposition to *Kara-uta*, "Chinese poetry." This preface was written at a time when Japan as a culture had already adopted Chinese characters. Official documents were written almost entirely in Chinese, and Chinese poetry was studied with just as much fervor as it was in China itself. Nevertheless, Tsurayuki's determination to preserve the old tradition of *Yamato-uta* is clearly visible. This year marks precisely 1,100 years since the publication of the *Kokin wakashū*—a good opportunity to reflect anew on the linguistic inheritance bestowed on us by our ancestors.

(2005)

The Culture of Name Succession

When kabuki actor Ichikawa Ebizō XI formally succeeded to the name "Ebizō" in 2004, commemorative performances were staged not only around Japan but also as far away as Paris. I was not in Paris at the time, but I understand the show found favor with the critics. When I happened to visit that city the following year, a French friend of mine who had been in the audience shared his impressions with me.

The florid spectacle of the kabuki stage is always well received outside Japan, but what had interested my friend most about this event was seeing a crowd of actors in sumptuous costumes lined up on stage for the *kōjō* or "statement"—the official announcement that one of their fellows had changed his name. My friend had found this quite peculiar and indeed still seemed somewhat baffled by it. The tradition of *shūmei*, literally "succeeding to a name," had of course been explained at the event itself, but he still found it hard to accept completely.

In Western culture, it is true, popular actors simply do not cast aside the names they are widely known by and adopt others in their place. The superb performances of Edmund Kean were discussed in France for more than a century after his death, but no one would dream of declaring themselves "Kean II" or "Kean III." Names belong to individuals and die with their owners.

But things are different in Japan. Names like "Ebizō" and "Danjūrō" have an authority and gravity that transcend the individual. They derive their power from the successes achieved by the cumulative effort of every actor who has borne them before and from the public memory and opinion regarding those successes—put simply, from history. The custom of succeeding to names is a finely honed system for ensuring that this inheritance is passed down properly so that it can be enriched even more. This is how tradition takes form.

Treasuring the inheritance of the past and seeking to hand it down to the next generation in the form of tradition is something seen in every country, every people. But recognizing the special role of the name in that process seems to me highly unique to Japan. The Japanese have always placed great importance on names. To say that something "has a name" (*na ga aru*) is to praise it as highly valuable. *Meibutsu* is often translated "famous thing," but literally means "thing with a name." There is no shortage of similar terms: *meijin* for a person preeminent in their field, *meisaku* for a superior work of art, *meihin* for a praiseworthy item, *meisan* for a renowned mountain. In many cases these terms are connected to the bequest of the past.

Consider the term *meisho*, "famous place." To become a *meisho*, natural beauty or noteworthy scenery is required—but that is not all. As shown by the profusion of *meisho-e* and *meisho-ka* (pictures and poems, respectively, of *meisho*), such places are visited by a wide variety of people who then depict them in art, praise them in poems, or include them in stories. The cumulative result of these efforts creates the value of the *meisho*.

We might say, then, that Ebizō's performance in Paris was about more than simply announcing the arrival of a brilliant actor. It was also an attempt to convey part of what makes Japanese culture unique.

(2005)

The Aesthetics of the Margin

The tale of tea-ceremony master Sen no Rikyū and the morning glories is well known. The full story can be found in the previous section of this book, but the outlines are simple enough to repeat here. When Toyotomi Hideyoshi came to see Rikyū's famous garden of morning glories, he was dismayed and angered to find that Rikyū had plucked every flower in the garden before his arrival. However, upon entering Rikyū's tea-ceremony room, Hideyoshi saw that a single morning glory bloom had been arranged in the *tokonoma* alcove, and this was more than enough to satisfy him.

This story is a good illustration of Rikyū's philosophy of beauty. A garden full of morning glories in bloom is, of course, an appealing scene in its own right. But Rikyū sacrificed that beauty to concentrate it all into a single point in the *tokonoma*. To heighten the impact of a single flower's beauty, all the other flowers are unnecessary—in fact, they only get in the way. The excision of unnecessary and unwanted elements is what allows Rikyū's aesthetics to take form.

However, picking all the flowers in the garden was not simply about eliminating the unnecessary. The bare garden played an important role in forming the aesthetic world Hideyoshi entered that day. The high expectations he brought with him were dashed when he saw the empty garden. He surely still felt that disappointment as he entered the tea-ceremony room, and coming face-to-face with the flower in the *tokonoma* in that state was a much greater shock than simply seeing a single flower with no particular meaning would have been. The deeper his initial dissatisfaction, the bigger the surprise, and the more powerful the impression left. This, we may be sure, was all part of Rikyū's plan.

The flower in the tea-ceremony room, highlighted by the absence of flowers in the garden: to create an aesthetic world like this in a painting, simply placing a flower at the center of the tableau would not be enough. The composition would need a flower on one side and, on the other side, empty space—exactly the kind of space created by the margins in Japanese ink wash painting.

The word *margin* here corresponds to *yohaku* in Japanese. This word is difficult to translate into English or French, but literally means "leftover blank." In Western oil painting, be it landscape or still life, the entire canvas is expected to be covered in paint, corner to corner: a bare patch with nothing painted on it would be viewed as an incomplete section. But in a Japanese work like Hasegawa Tōhaku's *Pine Trees*, between the stands of dark pines and the stands of pines so light they seem to be fading away, there is a space containing nothing at all. It is this space that gives the painting its mystical depth; the atmosphere of the painting seems to come from the empty space itself. Similarly, in *Landscape* (p. 162), painted in the abbot's quarters (*hōjō*) at Daitokuji by Kanō Tan'yū, the broad, empty margin confronts the viewer almost as if it were the main motif of the painting.

Hasegawa Tōhaku, *Pine Trees* (*Shōrin-zu*), Azuchi-Momoyama period.
Tokyo National Museum.

The total elimination of whatever is unnecessary or secondary has always been a key characteristic of the Japanese aesthetic consciousness. The courtyard before the Shishinden (throne room) at Kyoto Imperial Palace has none of the flowerbeds or statues or fountains you might see at a Western palace. Instead, the ground is covered in white gravel and the space is left empty and pure. Similarly, the Ise Grand Shrine, with its unpainted wood construction devoid of all ornamentation or color, has been maintained in its original form since its founding and remains vibrant today.

The practice of regularly rebuilding the Ise Grand Shrine is said to have begun in the second half of the seventh century, and its current form is said to date from that period, too. At that time, Buddhism had more than a century of history in Japan, and colorful Buddhist temple architecture could be seen at many sites around the country—particularly the capital, Nara, which poets praised for its beauty "in red and green." With tiled roofs and base stones under their pillars, these temples were also the result of more advanced construction methods, making them much more likely to be preserved than the earthfast pillars and thatched roof of the Ise Grand Shrine (which, indeed, is why the shrine must be rebuilt every twenty years). We know that the builders of the Ise Grand Shrine were not unaware of these new techniques from the continent, for a Buddhist influ-

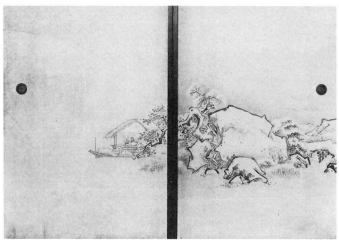

Kanō Tan'yū, *Landscape* (*Sansui-zu*), 1641. Daitokuji Temple.

ence can be detected in details like the surrounding railings (*kōran*). Nevertheless, the shrine was constructed in the old, simple style, and the Japanese people have preserved it in that style for over 1,300 years. The Japanese aesthetic of rejecting the unnecessary—an aesthetic deeply linked to spiritual beliefs—runs through this history in an unbroken line.

Of course, an aesthetic consciousness hungry for splendor and color is also a major characteristic of the Japanese, as the rise of Buddhist art shows. It has often been observed in the context of Japanese art history that along with the ink wash paintings discussed above we also find the gold fields and rich coloring of *Yamato-e*, the classical Japanese painting style of the Heian period, and the gorgeous genre pictures of the early modern period. Indeed, in China, where ink wash painting was first developed, Japanese art was apparently considered decorative to the point of flamboyance. The early twelfth century *Xuanhe Manual of Painting* (*Xuanhe huapu*), the first known commentary on Japanese art by a non-Japanese author, says of the Japanese pictures in the collection of Emperor Huizong of Song that "the coloring is extremely heavy, with gold and blue used in great quantity." We do not know exactly which works the art-loving Emperor had obtained, but they were clearly exquisitely decorated, in stark contrast to the austerity of ink wash paintings.

Even in the most dazzling, florid works of Japanese art, however, we can detect a strong tendency to exclude everything outside the central motif. Consider the well-known *Irises* (p. 77) by Ogata Kōrin. A Western artist painting irises blooming by a river would seek to recreate the scene in its entirety: the surface of the pond, the riverbank, the meadow, probably even the clouds in the sky. I have even been asked by a Westerner exactly where these irises are supposed to be blooming. But just as Rikyū cleared his garden of flowers, Kōrin has eliminated all peripheral elements from his painting and replaced them with a gorgeous field of gold. This gold field is both a way of covering up unnecessary elements and a background in and of itself.

Similarly, consider the countless "In and around the capital" (*rakuchū rakugai*) paintings of the early modern period (p. 104). These works depict a range of famous places, from Nijō Castle to the many shrines and temples of Kyoto, as well as various streetscapes, events, and observances. All

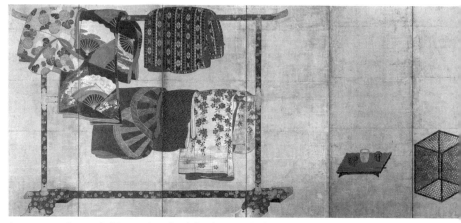

Anonymous, *Tagasode* (*Tagasode-zu byōbu*), Edo period. Idemitsu Museum of Arts.

of these, however, are surrounded by a decorative cloud-shaped motif, so that we seem to be looking down on Kyoto from above the clouds. The result is that the streets of the capital appear to be filled with drifting "golden clouds"—something else I am often asked about by Westerners. But it is precisely because these images are bordered by clouds, with intermediate areas covered up, that we can clearly tell what each individual part of the picture depicts.

As an example of this technique applied to interior scenes, consider the *tagasode* (literally "Whose sleeves?") genre. These paintings take women's kimonos on clothing racks as their main motif, but no attempt is made to depict the rooms in which the racks are placed—no walls, no floor, nothing at all. Sometimes the picture includes props implying a human presence—*sugoroku* boards, teacups on trays—but the people who might use these props are omitted. The technique of implying presence through absence is so common in Japanese art that it even has its own, rather elegant name: *rusu moyō*, roughly "visible absence." Instead of people, what takes the stage in these paintings is the familiar gold field.

In all of these cases, the fields or clouds of gold are, of course, ornamental, but they are also functional, covering up what is unnecessary for the composition. To return to the terminology discussed earlier, they are golden *yohaku*.

Even today, gold screens are often arranged at wedding receptions and other celebrations in Japan. But these screens are always plain gold. When I attended a party at the Japanese Embassy in Seoul late last year, a gold screen had been erected near the entrance, and the ambassador stood before this to welcome guests as the arrived. A Korean friend I was with remarked at how Japanese the scene was. My curiosity aroused, I asked what my friend meant, and learned that, while gold screens are often deployed at Korean celebrations, in Korea the screen will always have a vivid fortuitous motif on it as well: a pine tree, perhaps, or a crane. To my friend, a plain gold screen seemed to be lacking something, even to have a melancholy, lonely air. One nation's melancholy, however, is another's simplicity. Look closely at a field of plain gold, and the Japanese aesthetic consciousness begins to come into view.

(2006)

Postcards and Place

Whenever I visit a place for the first time, in Japan or elsewhere, I make a point of buying a postcard. Postcards make good souvenirs, but that is not the only reason I buy them. The fact is that postcards can convey all kinds of information to the careful observer.

For example, when arriving in a new town where one doesn't know west from east, a glance at the postcards on display in any nearby souvenir shop will give a fair idea of the main local sightseeing spots. The buildings depicted on postcards are usually quite noticeable, so they make excellent landmarks for visitors roaming the streets. In the case of very large structures like cathedrals, high-up details that are difficult to see from street level are quite clear on postcards. The famous gargoyles and chimeras that haunt the Galerie des chimères at the front of Notre-Dame Cathedral in Paris were up too high to make out properly from the ground, but when I visited a nearby souvenir shop I saw their oddly appealing faces lined up in a row—testament to the power of the postcard.

I had a similar experience on a recent visit to Pavia, a small town about an hour's drive from Milan in northern Italy. Pavia has a population of just 70,000, but its long and distinguished history dates back to medieval times and remains palpable today in its many churches and castles. Particularly noteworthy is the Certosa, a towering monastery on a plot of land on the outskirts of the main urban center. The Certosa's façade is covered with carvings of plant motifs, human figures, and scenes from stories; within the annals of art history, it is a masterpiece of unparalleled extravagance. On the day of my visit, the south half of the building happened to be covered up for repairs, but even in this state, the exuberance of the imagery was stunning.

There is an abundance of frescos, reliefs, and altars to be found inside the Certosa as well, but what particularly delighted me—along with my fellow sightseers—was a picture painted high on the rear wall of the nave, depicting a monk leaning in through a window to peer down at us. As evidence of the playful spirit of the Certosa's builders, this *trompe-l'œil*, was of great interest, but the sheer distance of the painting from the floor made its fine details impossible to see clearly. While this did add to the effect, I found it frustrating. Fortunately, the gift shop in the church sold a postcard featuring the monk in close-up, as well as one showing the building's complete façade. I bought both.

As I collected postcards from my travels, I noticed that they all tend to present their subjects the same way. From the Certosa in Pavia to the Coliseum in Rome or the Arc de Triomphe in Paris, postcards from the West center landmarks in the frame and exclude the surroundings as much as possible. This may seem perfectly natural given that the goal of these postcards is to introduce sightseeing spots, but it is not the only possible approach. In Japan, it is very rare for a postcard to show a building alone, be it temple or castle.

Postcard from Certosa monastery in Pavia.

Glancing through my postcards from Kyoto, I find that the overwhelming majority depict buildings and their natural surroundings together, as unified entities: scenes like "Kinkakuji in the Snow," depicting the temple and its gardens blanketed in white, and "Spring at Kiyomizudera," which foregrounds the cherry blossoms rather than the building. The same nature that would be eliminated from postcards in the West plays a leading role in the Japanese equivalent.

This is closely connected to how the Japanese conceive of "famous places" (*meisho*) as well as their views of nature. *Meisho* were originally understood to include the natural world, like the autumn foliage of Mount Takao or the enormous Daigo-Sakura tree. This is even clearer in the *meisho* ukiyo-e that served the function of today's postcards before the advent of photography.

Hiroshige's late work *One Hundred Famous Views of Edo* is one such example. This was a series of ukiyo-e depicting Edo *meisho*, just as the title says, published one after another until Hiroshige's death. By then, the series had reached 118 views; Hiroshige's publisher added another, included a cover illustration, and published the result as a set of 120. The publisher

Utagawa Hiroshige, "View to the North from Mount Asuka" (Asukayama, kita no chōbō) from *One Hundred Famous Views of Edo* (*Meisho Edo hyakkei*), 1856.

also took the opportunity to group the prints by season. They had not had any particular organizing principle originally, but each one had a seasonal connection of some sort: fine weather after snow at Nihonbashi, spring flowers at Mount Asuka, and so on. These seasonal themes were not limited to natural phenomena; events like the raising of carp streamers in May, the Tanabata festival in July, and the summer fireworks at Ryōgoku also made an appearance. In Hiroshige's series, *meisho* consist of not just places but places combined with times—indeed, with the cycle of time itself.

In the West, though, monuments like the Arc de Triomphe and the great cathedrals are built to transcend the cycles of nature and the passage of time to last forever. The very word *monument* ultimately goes back to the Latin verb *monēre*, "to remind": monuments are built to commemorate events and convey those memories to generations far into the future. They might be called mechanisms for ensuring the inheritance of memory. Memories of events tend to be forgotten and lost once the people involved pass on, and monuments are a way of struggling against that forgetting, since hard stone does not slip away so easily.

The Japanese value memories too, of course. But since ancient times, they have sought their guarantee of memory's inheritance in the passage of nature rather than the hardness of stone. Nature does not stand in opposition to humanity; on the contrary, it is something humans rely on.

This is also apparent in each side's approach to urban planning. Western monuments like the Arc de Triomphe, Berlin's Victory Column, and major churches also function as landmarks. This is why they are often constructed on a grand scale. In Japan, the landmarks are natural ones: in Kyoto, the Higashiyama hills to the east; in Nara, the Ikoma hills. The same was true of Edo—not one of Hiroshige's *Views* depicts a lone building as the "star." The landmarks that do appear pointedly and repeatedly are Mount Fuji and Mount Tsukuba. As suggested by the inclusion in the classic Kabuki play *The Scabbard Crossing* (*Sayaate*) of the line "To the west, Fuji; to the north, Tsukuba," Edoites spent their entire day, from morning to night, conscious of their proximity to these mountains. The streetscape "Suruga-chō" in Hiroshige's *Hundred Famous Views* shows a lengthwise view of the street, which extends into the background according to the techniques of Western perspective. Rising above it all, like a great umbrella, is Mount Fuji—but it should not be concluded that Mount Fuji happened to be visible when glancing down the street. The street itself was laid out in a direction that would allow Mount Fuji to be seen. Such was the closeness felt by the people of Edo to the mountain.

From *meisho* ukiyo-e to the postcards that serve a similar function today, the differences between depictions in the East and the West clearly articulate the underlying difference in views of nature and aesthetic consciousness.

(2006)

Gagaku Without Gagaku

It was common a few decades ago, and is not unheard-of today, to hear Japan disparaged as a nation of imitators—a people with a knack for adopting and adapting foreign inventions but lacking the creativity to come up with their own. It is true that, from ancient times, Japan learned and received much from China; since the early modern period, it has learned from the West as well. But, while receptiveness to foreign cultures may be imitative, it does not necessarily imply a lack of creativity. Imitation can take many forms. Japan did not simply seize every fruit within reach from the advanced cultures it encountered. Certain aspects of those cultures that Japan was surely familiar with were nevertheless ignored. In the process of adopting foreign ideas, some form of selective decision-making was clearly at work, and it is here that we can discern what distinguishes Japan from other countries and makes it unique.

In his book *What Are the Japanese?* (*Nihonjin to wa nani ka*; PHP Kenkyūsho, 1989), Yamamoto Shichihei addresses this issue, offering a litany of Chinese customs and ideas that Japan did not imitate: "Imperial examinations, eunuchs, exogamy, polygyny, family names (*xing*), tributary states, the concept of the 'Mandate of Heaven' and the revolts it licensed, and, somewhat later, foot-binding." Every item on this list once played an important role in China—some still play such a role today—and all are directly related to the essence of Chinese culture. Neighboring Korea accepted that culture unchanged, so the ideas on this list were present on the Korean Peninsula as well; nevertheless, they failed to cross the waters to

Japan. The question Yamamoto poses in his book's title cannot be answered without addressing this issue.

Political order, philosophy, and societal custom are closely intertwined by nature. Excising any one of these inevitably affects the others. Japan's ancient *ritsuryō* legal system, for example, was imported from China, but according to Yamamoto it was "a *ritsuryō* system with neither Mandate of Heaven nor imperial examinations," making it quite unlike its original Chinese model. Japan's rejection of both exogamy and the imperial examination system, Yamamoto argues, was "ultimately a rejection of the fundamentals of [Chinese] social and political order."

Similar observations have been made in other fields. For example, another cultural product that was not transmitted to (or, put more bluntly, was rejected by) Japan was the imperial court music *yayue* known as *gagaku* in Japanese.

This assertion invites immediate protest. *Gagaku* was not rejected at all, an objector might say; as a musical tradition, it was transmitted safely across the waters. I had assumed the same thing, albeit without ever giving the matter much thought. But the truth is not so simple.

Kido Toshirō examines this topic from a variety of angles in his book *Young Antiquity* (*Wakaki kodai*; Shunjūsha, 2006). Kido is both the long-time leader of the National Theatre of Japan's project of reconstructing ancient instruments like the *kugo*, and a researcher and lecturer on topics such as *gagaku*, *mikagura* (ritual Shinto music), and *shōmyō* (Buddhist chanting). As the subtitle "Essays on the Rediscovery of Japanese Culture" (*Nihon bunka saihakken shiron*) suggests, in the book he offers perceptive observations on more than just music, exploring everything from painting and crafts to architecture and landscaping. What he has to say about *gagaku* can be summarized as follows.

It is true that the *gagaku* preserved even today by the Music Department of the Imperial Household Agency's Board of Ceremonies was brought to Japan from China roughly 1,300 years ago. The Chinese word *yayue* was borrowed as *gagaku* at that time to name the music, and Japan even established a "*Gagaku* Department" (*Gagaku-ryō*) in imitation of the Tang dynasty's practices—although, as Kido notes, the department was known in Japanese as the "Office of Song and Dance" (*uta-mai no tsukasa*).

However, despite its name, the *Gagaku* Department did not practice the original *yayue* of China. Instead, its musicians performed "banquet music" (*yanyue*)—music for entertainment—and "barbarian music" (*huyue*) from central Asia. These genres are understood to be included in the word *gagaku* today, but at the time they were known in Japanese as *rin'yūgaku* (literally "Champan music," referring to an area in what is today central and southern Vietnam) and *komagaku* ("Korean music"), or, collectively, as *reigaku* ("performers' music")—they were not called *gagaku* at all. The original *yayue* of the Tang dynasty was the ceremonial Confucian music of the state, and this was not transmitted to Japan. As Yamamoto Shichihei might put it, Japan received "a *gagaku* without ceremonial Confucian music"—a *gagaku* without *gagaku*.

Why should this be the case? Kido argues that it was because "Japan already had its own religion, Shinto, and an associated ritual music, *mikagura*." The rejection of *yayue* was intentional.

This is a position worth considering. It implies a Japan whose apparent willingness to embrace whatever arrives from the outside world actually conceals a sense of resistance, along with the selectivity to reject whatever offends that sense. A similar mechanism can be seen at work in Japan's adoption of the *ritsuryō* system but not imperial examinations or eunuchs, and no doubt in other areas as well. In aggregate, these rejections can surely shed light on the essential characteristics of Japan and its people.

The Shinto ritual music of *mikagura* is explored in detail in Kido's book, and his discussion of not only its forms of expression but also the underlying philosophy supporting those forms—and how it compares to that of Western music—is both stimulating and intriguing. Kido observes, for example, that while virtually all Western music unfolds within the flow of time, in *mikagura* as in East Asian music in general time and space are not distinguished; sounds simply accumulate in space. This opens new perspectives on not only musical expression but also other fields like architecture and painting. Kido disagrees strongly with the current tendency to treat the music of the West as the only correct standard for music, and in this respect, too, his work is truly a valuable contribution towards the "rediscovery of Japanese culture."

(2007)

Canonical Beauty and Situational Beauty

Some time ago now, I heard an interesting story from a professor of agriculture.

While studying in the United States, he learned about a research project exploring people's views of animals. Participants were asked to answer questions like "What is the most beautiful animal?", and the results were scrutinized for differences by age, sex, occupation, religion, ethnicity, and so on.

Intrigued by this idea, the professor decided to carry out the same survey in Japan. If all went well, he thought, it could be developed into a comparative cultural study of the two countries. Soon, however, he ran into unforeseen difficulties.

When participants in the United States were asked what the most beautiful animal was, they would respond immediately with something like "Horse" or "Lion." But getting an answer was more difficult in Japan. "Hmm," participants would say. "That's a good question." If pressed, they would offer a response like "Let me see … maybe a flock of birds taking wing against the sunset?"

Eventually, the professor gave up. "I realized that any sort of comparison would be impossible," he told me with a rueful smile.

What intrigued me about this story was not what it suggested about views of animals in Japan versus the United States, but rather the way it highlighted a difference in aesthetic consciousness between Japanese people and Americans.

In the West, the prevailing opinion since ancient Greece has found beauty in things with a clear order to them. That order might take many forms—bilateral symmetry, proportionality between part and whole, affinity with some fundamental geometric form—but it is always based on objective principles, and it is beauty's ultimate source. Put the other way, a work that is created based on principles of this sort must express beauty.

Consider the idea, still common today, that the most beautiful human form is eight heads tall. This notion dates back to fourth-century BCE Greece, where such principles were called *canons*. Canons were not set in stone: even in Greece, a stocky seven heads was considered a more "canonical" height than a lithe eight in the previous century. But while the ideal itself might change, the underlying view that beauty arose from principles did not. The appeal of Greek sculpture derives in large part from these aesthetics.

Most of the sculpture from this period has, of course, been lost. The bulk of what is left to us today actually consists of copies from the age of Imperial Rome. But, even through these often imperfect copies, we can discern the forms of the originals to a great extent, and this is because of the canons they embodied. Insofar as they were created based on these principles of beauty, beauty was what these sculptures expressed.

But the Japanese aesthetic consciousness has little interest in grasping beauty through physical form. Since ancient times, the Japanese have been less interested in *what* is beautiful than the *circumstances* in which beauty is born. Instead of the "canonical beauty" of the West, the focus has been on what we might call "situational beauty."

Consider the famous haiku by Matsuo Bashō:

furuike ya	old pond
kawazu tobikomu	frog jumps in
mizu no oto	sound of water

Bashō did not call the pond or frog beautiful, or praise the "sound of water" as exquisite. He discovered an entirely new beauty in the world of deep silence, pregnant with tension, just as the frog jumped into the pond. That beauty had no physical form; it was purely situational.

One of the best examples of this aesthetic consciousness in action is the famous opening of Sei Shōnagon's *Pillow Book* "In spring it is the dawn. The gradually whitening mountains grow brighter at the edges. ..." With this keen sensitivity, the passage identifies the most beautiful time of day in each of the four seasons in turn—the epitome of situational beauty. For example:

> In autumn it is the evening. As the setting sun reaches the edge of the mountains, the crows return to their roosts in threes and fours, twos and threes, and even their hurried flight is moving. The lines of wild geese far overhead look elegantly small. ...

This connects directly to the modern aesthetic consciousness that favors a "flock of birds taking wing against the sunset." The sensibilities of the Japanese have remained alive and unchanged for over a thousand years.

Because canonical beauty is expressed in the thing itself, it can exist at any time and place, regardless of the circumstance. The Venus de Milo was created in the first century BCE in a Greek colonial outpost on a Mediterranean island, but it is no less beautiful on display in Paris's Louvre museum today. Even dropped into the middle of a desert, its beauty would be just as compelling.

But this is not so for situational beauty, which is, of course, lost if the situation changes. The beauty of a spring dawn or an autumn evening is fleeting. The Japanese sensitivity to situational beauty is precisely what cultivated the view of beauty as something temporary and unstable rather than eternally fixed.

This is also what lies behind the Japanese fondness, from ancient times to the present day, for events which celebrate the natural beauty of the season, from cherry blossom viewing in spring to moon viewing in autumn. As Sei Shōnagon demonstrates with penetrating accuracy, to the Japanese, beauty is inextricably linked to the change of seasons and the passage of time—in short, to the workings of nature. This is also apparent in the *meisho-e* or "pictures of famous places" that enjoyed widespread popularity in the Edo period.

As the name suggests, *meisho-e* depicted must-see sights and destinations from around Japan. But they did not simply depict physical locations. For example, Hiroshige's late masterpiece *One Hundred Famous Views of Edo* includes such scenes as fine weather after snow at Nihonbashi and Mount Asuka covered in spring flowers (p. 168)—each image depicts place and season as a single entity. It is worth noting that when Hiroshige's publisher first collected this series for posthumous republication as a complete set, he was able to divide the pictures into four seasonal groups even though Hiroshige had not drawn them based on any such scheme. Hiroshige had simply depicted the sights of Edo as they occurred to him, in more or less random order, but each one was inextricably combined with a particular season or observance, and this made the posthumous categorization by season possible. Put another way, *meisho* themselves—the "famous places" depicted in *meisho-e*—were born of the connection between Edo streetscapes and nature.

In many ways, postcards are the modern equivalent of *meisho-e*. In places like Paris and Rome, the postcards that fill the souvenir shops tend to depict representative monuments: the Notre-Dame Cathedral, the Arc de Triomphe, the Eiffel Tower. The overwhelming majority of Japanese postcards, however, depict scenes clad in seasonal garb: Kiyomizudera under the cherry blossoms in full bloom, Kinkakuji blanketed in snow. Of course, both Kiyomizudera and Kinkakuji are splendid buildings in their own right, but photographers for postcards prefer to combine that beauty with the changing season when recording it for posterity. This is yet another expression of the fondness for situational beauty in the Japanese aesthetic consciousness.

(2007)

Taikan and Fuji

In 2008, the National Art Center in Roppongi, Tokyo, commemorated the fiftieth anniversary of Yokoyama Taikan's death with a major retrospective of his work. Taikan was a giant of modern Japanese painting whose life spanned the Meiji, Taishō, and Shōwa eras. The exhibition included both celebrated masterworks and seldom-seen rarities, some on loan from overseas collections. As I neared the end of the exhibit, I paused before one work hung near the exit: Taikan's late masterpiece, *A Day in the Pacific Ocean* (p. 180, top left).

The painting depicts an ocean that rises from the bottom and then splits into two parts, left and right, beneath a cloud run through with eerie lightning. A fierce billowing fills the tableau, and a dragon writhes in agony as it struggles to escape from between the seething waves. Its sights are set on a calm, beautiful form far in the distance towards the top of the painting: Mount Fuji.

Taikan was so fond of using this sacred peak as a motif in his paintings that he is sometimes known as the "Painter of Fuji." He is said to have depicted the mountain in more than a thousand works over the course of his life, if sketches are included in the count. But even among this vast oeuvre, it is unusual to see the mountain over an ocean displaying such ferocious violence. What was in Taikan's heart when he painted this work, combining a madly raging Pacific and a placid Mount Fuji?

To Taikan, Mount Fuji had always been a symbol of his homeland of Japan. His great work *Japan, Land of the Rising Sun* (*Hi izuru tokoro Nihon*) is a representative example. Painted in 1940 for an exhibition celebrating Imperial Year 2600 (based on the traditional dates of the first Japanese emperor's reign, the Imperial Year system was abandoned after the end of World War II), *Japan, Land of the Rising Sun* was presented to the Emperor and remains among the holdings of the Imperial Household Agency's Sannomaru Shōzōkan. The painting shows a refined and dignified Mount Fuji on the left bathed in the red light of sun on the right; fresh and invigorating, the work is a masterpiece.

But Taikan felt that the Japan he depicted in such works expired in the war. In a document thought to be a draft for his 1946 New Year's address at the Japan Art Institute (Nippon Bijutsuin), Taikan speaks of a "Pacific without Japan":

> A history of three thousand years is annihilated; at the prospect of a Pacific without Japan, our emotion is immeasurable. But it is precisely because the arts of East Asia retain their strength that they shall play a leading role in the establishment of a new Japan, which shall once more stride confidently onto the world stage—thus do I believe.
>
> (Quoted in the catalog for the 2008 exhibition *Yokoyama Taikan Fifty Years On* [*Botsugo gojūnen Yokoyama Taikan*])

Taikan believed that his native land had died and could only be revived through the power of art. He was also determined to shoulder the responsibility of this art-based reconstruction himself.

A Day in the Pacific Ocean was painted and shown at the Japan Art Institute's fall exhibition in 1952. This was the year that the Peace Treaty of San Francisco came into effect after its signing in 1951, releasing Japan from Allied occupation and restoring its independence. Taikan must have been deeply moved to see his homeland finally embark on its journey towards rebirth, less than a decade after it had been reduced to ruins. The dragon striving to escape the raging waves surely represents the struggle for reconstruction, and Mount Fuji towering in the distance can only symbolize the "new Japan." Taikan's work was always sensitive to the changing times, and in this particular piece, which accosts the viewer with striking force, we sense the painter laying his heart bare on the canvas.

Katsushika Hokusai, *Dragon Rising over Mount Fuji* (*Fujigoe no ryū-zu*), 1849. Hokusai-kan.

Yokoyama Taikan, *A Day in the Pacific Ocean* (*Aru hi no taiheiyō*), 1952. National Museum of Modern Art, Tokyo. (See plate 19)

Yokoyama Taikan, *Cranes Flying Past the Divine Peak* (*Reihō hikaku*), 1953. Yokoyama Taikan Memorial Hall.

To realize his unique conceptions, it was inevitable that Taikan would study Japan's traditions deeply and incorporate them into his creative output. The link between Mount Fuji and dragons was not his own invention, and *A Day in the Pacific Ocean* was not the first work to depict it. On the contrary, the belief that a divine dragon resided in the sacred mountain had been widespread since the Edo period, and many painters took up the theme of Mount Fuji and its dragon. One well-known example is the late masterpiece by Katsushika Hokusai, *Dragon Rising over Mount Fuji* (p. 180, top right). In this work, a dragon that likely represents Hokusai himself soars over the mountain's peak on its way to the heavens.

When Yamashita Yoshiya of the Shizuoka Prefectural Museum of Art surveyed examples of the "Dragon over Fuji" genre, he found that the first to incorporate this theme clearly into a painting was Kanō Tan'yū, who was in turn likely inspired by a Chinese poem in seven-character quatrain form (*qiyan jueju*) written by Tan'yū's friend Ishikawa Jōzan:

仙客来遊雲外巓	Immortals come to frolic on the peak above the clouds;
神龍栖老洞中淵	The divine dragon has long brooded in the caves' watery deeps.
雪如紈素煙如柄	Snow like glossy white silk, smoke like a handle;
白扇倒懸東海天	A white fan hung upended in the sky, above the eastern sea.

Jōzan's poem apparently enjoyed widespread popularity among artists and literati. Even the Meiji painter Tomioka Tessai produced work inspired by it.

As the poem suggests, there was also a long tradition of seeing Mount Fuji as a gathering spot for the immortals of Taoist legend. The Heian writer Miyako no Yoshika recorded (whether truly or otherwise) that two beautifully adorned immortal maidens were seen dancing elegantly on the peak of Mount Fuji by an enormous crowd of witnesses. The mountain is also present in the background of the popular Noh play *The Feathered Robe* (*Hagoromo*), in which a celestial maiden dances for a fisherman. The first line of Jōzan's poem is generally interpreted as a reference to these legends.

But this is not the only possible interpretation. In a paper I happened to run across, a young scholar argued that this word for "immortal" can also refer metaphorically to cranes, in which case Jōzan's poem would invoke the image of a flock of cranes circling the mountain.

Cranes are an auspicious symbol in Japan, and Mount Fuji is thought to grant good fortune, too. (There is a folk belief dating from the Edo period that Mount Fuji is the most desirable thing to see in your first dream of the year. The second-best thing to see is an eagle, and in third place is an eggplant.) In other words, just as the concept of divinity links Mount Fuji and the dragon, Mount Fuji and the crane are linked by their auspicious nature.

This interpretation certainly seems worthy of consideration, partly because there is no shortage of paintings depicting Mount Fuji and cranes in combination. For example, the eighteenth-century painter Nagasawa Rosetsu's *Cranes Passing Mount Fuji* (*Fujigoe tsuru-zu*) depicts a line of cranes flying tranquilly past the towering mountain. The Sannomaru Shōzōkan also holds a set of six-panel folding screens entitled *Cranes Flying Past the Divine Peak* (*Reihō hikaku*) by modern painter Dōmoto Inshō. Two large cranes soaring into the heavens are painted on the right screen, and Mount Fuji can be seen in the distance beyond Mount Ashitaka—an auspicious scene of true refinement and beauty.

It is interesting to note that in the year after painting *A Day in the Pacific Ocean*, Taikan created his own painting with the title *Cranes Flying Past the Divine Peak* (p. 180, bottom). At the Taikan retrospective, these two paintings were arranged side-by-side, and the contrast with the dark and turbulent *A Day in the Pacific Ocean* highlighted the world of boundless quiet and peace depicted in *Cranes Flying Past the Divine Peak*, with its graceful and dignified Mount Fuji surrounded by scattered flocks of cranes in the bright morning sun. This, too, was one of the ways Taikan saw Mount Fuji—or perhaps he was dreaming of the shape of things to come for Japan.

(2008)

Whither *Passing Spring?*

I recently had a surprising experience at the Aichi Prefectural Museum of Art exhibition *Utopia of Images and Letters: Japanese Modern Art and Art Magazines, 1889–1915* (*Shijō no yūtopia: Kindai Nihon no kaiga to bijutsu zasshi 1889–1915*). True to its subtitle, the exhibition included a variety of art magazines, illustrations, prints, and other images from around the turn of the century—including, to my surprise, Aoki Shigeru's painting *Passing Spring* (*Yuku haru*). I had been intrigued by this somewhat puzzling work and its mysteries for some time, but this unexpected encounter was the first time I had seen it in person, and I found myself transfixed by it for some time.

The painting depicts a woman in Japanese dress sitting in a chair with a Japanese zither called a *koto* balanced on her lap. Her hands hesitantly touch the strings, but she does not seem about to perform: her distant gaze and brooding look indicate that her thoughts are elsewhere. The woman's oval face and long hair reflect Aoki's tastes, as do the objects placed around her, which include a peacock's feather, an ancient Chinese lute known to-day as a *ruan*, a diagonal lattice screen, several volumes of the *Tale of Genji*. From the signature and date at the top of the painting are "S. Awoki/1906," anyone would assume that the painting was Aoki's work.

In fact, however, things are not that simple. The story of this painting appears to begin one year earlier, when a work with an identical title was displayed by Fukuda Tane at a 1905 exhibition held by the Pacific Painting Society. Fukuda's painting has been lost, but it is clear from photographs of the exhibition that the overall composition of the two works, including the arrangement of still-life objects around the subject, was basically identical. There were, however, some minor differences in the details of the subject's clothing, and above all the woman's face in Fukuda's painting was much rounder—not Aoki-like at all. These commonalities and differences have inspired a great deal of discussion, particularly on the question of Aoki's involvement.

A preliminary conclusion was reached when the Fuchū Art Museum, which owns Aoki's painting, performed a meticulous examination of it during a restoration project, even inspecting it via X-ray. Chief curator Shiga Hidetaka published a detailed analysis of these results in 1999. To summarize his conclusions, Shiga argues that after Fukuda Tane painted her *Passing Spring* and exhibited it at the Pacific Painting Society's exhibition, Aoki Shigeru made additions and modifications to that work: the *Passing Spring* we have today is, therefore, a collaboration between the two. As a result, at the *Utopia of Images and Letters* exhibition, the painting was attributed to "Aoki Shigeru/Fukuda Tane."

The work's place in art history poses some other interesting problems, such as its connection to the pre-Raphaelites, but what I wish to discuss here is its theme, and, in particular, its original inspiration. Standing before the painting at the museum, I suddenly wondered if I detected a shadow cast by the famous haiku by eighteenth-century poet and artist Yosa Buson:

yuku haru ya	passing spring
omotaki biwa no	this heavy *biwa* lute
dakigokoro	in my arms

The circumstantial details are different, of course. Whatever specific image Buson might have intended, it was certainly not a woman sitting in a chair. Above all, the woman in the painting is cradling a *koto*, not a *biwa*. But the title *Passing Spring* brought the haiku to mind almost reflexively all the same.

This may have something to do with my valued friend Haga Tōru's gem of a book *The Little World of Yosa Buson* (*Yosa Buson no chiisa na sekai*,

Chūōkōronsha, 1986), which impressed itself indelibly on my memory. Haga even includes a chapter entitled "This Heavy *Biwa* Lute" containing a detailed discussion of the lineage and meaning of the "passing spring" motif. Following an analysis of a poem by Bai Juyi and another by Bashō—

yuku haru ya	passing spring—
tori naki uo no	the birds cry, the fish
me wa namida	are teary-eyed

—Haga argues convincingly that while Buson was heir to these works, he opened an entirely new world of sensual beauty, perfumed with a sweet, somehow melancholy lethargy not seen in its predecessors. Bai, Bashō, Bu-

Fukuda Tane/Aoki Shigeru, *Passing Spring* (*Yuku haru*), 1906. Fuchū Art Museum.

son: each of these poets sang of their own unique world, but regret for the departing season resounds within the work of all three like a shared basso continuo. This regret, Haga says, is "a poetic sentiment clad in sensitive shadow, unique to the East." It might also be called an "aesthetics of passing," in opposition to the West's aesthetics of the eternal and unchanging. The "passing spring" motif invokes more than just the changing of the seasons—it is linked to an emotional world in which pathos, the famous Japanese *mono no aware*, is found even in that passing. Many great works of poetry have been born of that unique aesthetic consciousness.

The same is true of pictorial art. Spring is a common theme for Western painters, too, but tends to be expressed in the form of dazzling tableaus brimming with youth and vigor. It is difficult to recall even one painting that depicts spring as it departs, let alone with such deep pathos. Not so for Japanese painters, who have produced many such works.

The first one that occurred to me as I stood before Aoki's work in the museum was Takeuchi Seihō's *Regret for the Passing of Spring* (*Sekishun*). This painting is over four feet tall, with most of its space devoted to a simple, unremarkable heap of firewood. The pile is not even neatly arranged—the wood appears to have been piled up carelessly, and some has already fallen off and lies on the ground nearby. It is a blunt, unwelcoming motif, quite far from any poetic sentiment. But Seihō also scattered the tableau with tiny, pale pink petals, and atop the rough heap of wood he perched a full-grown warbler, known in Japan as the herald of spring. In concert with the petals that charmingly adorn the ground, this little bird presides over a late spring scene that is dreamlike, elegant, and sensual.

Then there is Kawai Gyokudō's *Passing Spring* (*Yuku haru*), now designated an Important Cultural Property. An enormous single painting covering two six-panel folding screens, this work depicts a valley stream with boatmen slowly poling their boats along against a verdant mountain backdrop. There are also countless falling petals, dancing and swirling across the entire tableau. This is precisely the world of Yoshida Kenkō's fourteenth-century *Essays in Idleness*: "Are flowers to be admired only in full bloom, the moon only when it is full?"

Aoki Shigeru and Fukuda Tane's *Passing Spring* inherits this tradition, this aesthetics of passing, no less surely. The work's title was probably selected by Aoki, a passionate lover of literature, and it can only have been the poems of Buson and Bashō and their predecessors that he had in mind. It is, after all, the fact that painting's subject is cradling an instrument that makes Buson's presence in the background so readily apprehensible.

As noted above, the instrument in the painting is a *koto* and not a *biwa* as in Buson's original. This may be because a *biwa* is more of the world of men. In Haga Tōru's estimation, Buson's haiku suggests a nobleman of some sort cradling the instrument. Some readers might have been reminded of the *biwa*-playing monks who recited the *Tale of the Heike*. Indeed, Kanokogi Takeshirō's masterpiece *Biwa Monk* (*Biwa hōshi*) was shown at the same Pacific Painting Society exhibition in 1905. In any case, if the *biwa* was of the world of men, it would hardly be unusual for Aoki to have his female subject cradle a *koto* instead. But this raises another question: why depict a female subject in the first place?

Before we answer that question, let us consider the unusual orthography in the title of the painting. There is often more than one way to write a word in Japanese, and this is the case for the word translated "passing" in this essay. It would normally be written using the Chinese character 行, literally just "go," but in the title of this painting it is written with the character 逝, implying something closer to "die." Bashō and Buson both used 行. It seems doubtful that any earlier poet would have used 逝, because, after all, it implies an eternal parting with no foreseeable reunion—quite unsuitable for the seasons, which repeat in a yearly cycle. Why did Fukuda Tane give such an unnatural name to the painting she submitted to an important exhibition?

In the paper mentioned earlier, Shiga Hidetaka offers an intriguing hypothesis. It seems that when Fukuda was working on the painting, she was twenty-one, and already pregnant with Aoki Shigeru's child. She was in the process of becoming a mother. The innocent days of her youth were coming to an end. The title of the work, Shiga concludes, was "an attempt to depict in classical tones a passionate unwillingness to leave her fleeting girlhood—a psychological self-portrait."

This interpretation of *Passing Spring* as a farewell to youth is entirely convincing. If the work is a self-portrait, then naturally its subject had to be female. This, in turn, meant changing the *biwa* was changed to a *koto*. Decades into the Meiji period, the "passing spring" motif that inspired so many of Japan's premodern poets had one more unforgettable song to sing.

(2008)

School Songs and Musical Education

In 2007, the Tokyo University of the Arts celebrated its 120th anniversary, its first incarnation, the Tokyo School of Fine Arts, having been founded in 1887. As it happens, the Tokyo Academy of Music was founded in the same year—but in terms of pedagogical policy, the two schools could not have been more different. The School of Fine Arts offered instruction only in traditional Japanese techniques; Western influences were resolutely excluded from every field, be it painting, sculpture, or handcrafts. By contrast, the Academy of Music was entirely receptive to Western music, reflecting the enthusiasm then current throughout society for *bunmei kaika* or "civilization and enlightenment," i.e. the cultural products of the West.

Several reasons for this difference can be identified. In the world of art, the Tokyo School of Fine Arts was preceded by the Technical Art School, founded in 1876 as the first art college established by the Meiji government. Antonio Fontanesi and two other Italian painters were invited to teach there as an experiment in the adoption of Western art in a fully Western fashion, but the school was forced to close down less than a decade later amid rising interest in reviving the old ways of Japan and increased importance placed on the opinions of foreign experts hired by the Meiji government, such as Ernest Fenollosa, who was drawn to the ancient arts of Japan and lobbied forcefully for their protection.

The world of music, however, had neither a Fontanesi nor a Fenollosa. The closest thing was probably Luther Whiting Mason, who arrived in Japan in 1879 at the behest of the Ministry of Education's Music Study

Committee. But Mason's stay in Japan was brief. Actively involved with the church from an early age, Mason sometimes set Japanese songs to hymnal tunes, and this led to suspicion that he was using music to evangelize the Christian religion. His employment was terminated during what was supposed to be a temporary visit home to the United States in 1882.

Despite the brevity of Mason's stay, however, he repeatedly stressed the importance of songs in school education, and the *Elementary School Song Book* (*Shōgaku shōkashū*), compiled by Mason and fellow committee member Isawa Shūji, was the first noteworthy fruit of the acceptance of Western music into Japan. This was a major achievement, not least because these "songs" (*shōka*) represented the first concretization of Western music for Japanese audiences.

In his commendable *School Songs and National Language: The Apparatus of Meiji Modernization* (*Shōka to kokugo: Meiji kindaika no sōchi*; Kōdansha, 2008), Santō Isao traces the background to and gestation of these songs, along with their later history, in detail. Santō offers an innovative perspective on his chosen topic, arguing that Mason and Isawa's project cannot be separated from the process of forming the "national language" (*kokugo*), which was ongoing at the same time.

The original goal of the Meiji government was to make Japan a "country of culture" (*bunmeikoku*) that could stand side-by-side with the developed nations of the West. To this end, it strove from an early date to establish political and social institutions on par with the West's. This was the "civilization and enlightenment" (*bunmei kaika*) mentioned above.

In 1872, the government announced plans for a national school system based on the lofty ideal of universal education: "No uneducated household in any village, no uneducated person in any home." The proposed subjects of study included "music" (*ongaku*) in lower elementary and "instrumental performance" (*sōgaku*) in middle elementary grades, but regarding the content of these subjects the plans were silent. And for good reason: without ready access to sheet music or instruments, just how Western music could be taught was far from clear. At the time, not only pianos but also organs and violins were all imported; the first Japan-made organ was not produced until 1887. All this made running a class in "instrumental performance" a tough proposition. The "singing" (*shōka*) format was established as a sort of last-minute compromise: the teacher would play an organ, and the students would sing along. Mason and Isawa's three-volume *Elementary School Song Book* was designed as a textbook for this class.

Last resort or not, the results of this approach were impressive, and the *Elementary School Song Book* made a considerable impact on Japanese musical culture. Many of the 91 songs in the text are still well-known and loved today, including "Open Them, Close Them" (Musunde hiraite), "By Firefly Light" (Hotaru no hikari), "Butterfly" (Chōchō), and "A Thousand Different Grasses in the Garden" (Niwa no chigusa). Some tunes made their first appearance with different names or lyrics than they have today; for example, "Open Them, Close Them," a simple hand game song all Japanese toddlers learn today, was originally called "Looking Out" (Miwataseba), and had lyrics about how the landscape changed with the seasons. Musically speaking, most of these songs were based on Spanish or Scottish folk tunes, but their continuing popularity shows that these borrowed melodies were nevertheless aligned with Japanese sensitivities. We can only admire the selective vision of the editors.

Lyrics, on the other hand, were composed chiefly by members of the Music Study Committee, who would send drafts to the Ministry of Education and Culture and receive corrections in return. Santō offers a close analysis of some of these interactions, finding that the Ministry's objections usually addressed content or language deemed unsuitable for educational material; the Committee members, no shrinking violets themselves, pushed back with appeals to musical effect or ease of singing, and fierce debate was sometimes the result. Most Committee members were actually also specialists in the pedagogy of the new "national language," and were furthermore of the "national learning" (*kokugaku*) school rooted in Japanese rather than Western tradition. This is interesting because the songs were, of course, connected to the problem of language.

After the publication of the *Elementary School Song Book*, many other songs were written for pedagogical purposes. At the same time, the "national language" was gradually being prepared. Santō's book traces in detail the process through which Japanese grammars, particularly "school grammars," were established based on Dutch and English models during the same period as the spread of school songs. In fact, school songs were also used *for* national language education, as well as to supplement lessons in geography and history, like Ōwada Takeki's well-known "railroad songs" (*tetsudō shōka*). It soon becomes clear that the national language was designed to unify the nation and the state while the school songs bore responsibility for spreading a shared national base of knowledge. This is what Santō means by the "apparatus of Meiji modernization."

The soprano Aikawa Yumi, in her book *Songs of Japan: Is This the Best We Can Do?* (*Kore de ii no ka, Nippon no uta*; Bungei Shunjū, 1998), makes an important point about the *Elementary School Song Book* which should not be overlooked. Regardless of the circumstances at the time, she argues, it was "fortunate" that music education in Japan's modern period began with *shōka*. First, because in Japan, music accompanying song or dance has traditionally been more developed than purely instrumental music— song almost always takes the leading role. And second, because of the enormous popularity throughout Japanese history of *kae-uta*, songs created by applying new lyrics to old tunes. Folk songs and other popular favorites always change or are created anew over their long transmissions, but Aikawa uses examples from lullabies and other folk music to show that in Japan such music is particularly prone to being changed to suit changing times or different geographical regions. Even hymns did not necessarily begin as religious music; many are created by replacing the lyrics of folk songs and favorites from around the world with poetry in praise of God. As a result, Mason and Isawa's offerings, which combined Japanese lyrics with Western folk tunes, were not considered unusual in the slightest, and, Aikawa concludes, "it was for this reason that Western music, which has no relation whatsoever to Japanese traditional music, was able to take root in Japan so quickly." In other words, even in the process of adopting Western musical practices, the traditional Japanese sensibility was at work.

It seems likely that this insightful observation is equally applicable to other domains, so that modernization in every field was made possible by traditional sensibilities. Indeed, perhaps a similar sort of active reception was at work in ancient times, too, when Japan first began to adopt the cultural products of continental Asia.

(2009)

Fukuzawa Yukichi, Traditionalist

At the *Fukuzawa Yukichi: Living the Future* (*Mirai o hiraku: Fukuzawa Yukichi*) exhibition held in 2009 at the Tokyo National Museum, I encountered a hanging scroll bearing a slogan in bold, generously sized characters: "The light of a country shines from its art." The words were in Fukuzawa's own hand, although the entire piece was a reproduction; the current whereabouts of the original, it seems, are unknown. Nor is it known exactly when Fukuzawa wrote this phrase, but it is nevertheless a concise representation of his thought.

The phrase "light of a country" here means a country's glory, its fame. It does not refer to political influence, or economic or military strength—or, at least, not those things alone. Kume Kunitake's account of the 1871–1873 Iwakura Mission to the prosperous, advanced nations of the West is preceded by a two-character calligraphic epigraph (*daiji*): 観光, *kankō*. In today's Japanese, this is simply the word for "sightseeing," but Kume is using it in an older sense, closer to its etymological meaning of "beholding the light"—the light of civilization itself.

What Fukuzawa means to say is that a country's level of civilization is embodied above all in its art. A similar idea can be found in Okakura Tenshin's editorial for the first issue of the arts magazine *Kokka*: "Art," Tenshin says, "is the flowering of the nation." (Indeed, the name of the magazine literally means "Flower of the nation".) Modern rationalist and promoter of "civilization and enlightenment" (*bunmei kaika*) on the model of the West though Fukuzawa was, in this respect his position is surprisingly close to that of Tenshin, who is often viewed as a conservative traditionalist.

We might also add that the word translated as "art" in the above paragraphs, *bijutsu*, was in Fukuzawa's time still new, and its meaning was highly fluid. In the Edo period and earlier, there had, of course, been many works of art, but the specific word *bijutsu* (and therefore the concept it refers to) had not yet been coined.

The word *bijutsu* made its first appearance in 1873, in the text of a notice urging participation in the Vienna World's Fair. Here it was meant to include not just painting and sculpture but also music and poetry (literature)—the broader category which in today's Japanese would be called *geijutsu*. But the scope of *bijutsu*'s meaning soon narrowed. Ernest Fenollosa's 1882 lecture "The Truth of *Bijutsu*" (Bijutsu shinsetsu) treated painting almost exclusively, and by the time the Tokyo School of Fine Arts (i.e. of *bijutsu*) was founded in 1887, the word's scope had stabilized to roughly its present broadness, indicating the plastic arts alone. We cannot be certain precisely what Fukuzawa meant by *bijutsu* when he took up his brush to write his slogan, but in any case he had the fruit of some creative artistic endeavor in mind.

How do we connect this position, which makes art the yardstick of a country's civilization, to Fukuzawa's advocacy of "enlightenment" in the form of the adoption of Western social systems and material culture?

Fukuzawa himself had absolutely no fondness for art or interest in collecting it. He says as much in his autobiography, describing himself as "artistically unaccomplished and incompetent, and, with the exception of calligraphy, entirely indifferent to antiquities and artworks." He also relates the tale of the single occasion on which he did buy a large quantity of art. The story is relatively well known, but, to summarize, Fukuzawa called on an acquaintance in Nihonbashi one day to find the living room filled with "a higgledy-piggledy arrangement of golden folding screens, *maki-e* lacquerware, vases, and the like." His acquaintance explained that the items were to be exported to the United States. There was not a single thing in the room that Fukuzawa himself wanted, but he nevertheless declared that he would buy the collection himself before he stood by and let it be sold off overseas. And that is exactly what he did, paying 2,200 or 2,300 yen for the lot—a considerable sum at the time.

In other words, Fukuzawa did not buy the artworks because he had fallen in love with them. Even after making the purchase, he spoke of the works extremely coldly. "I gained no pleasure from looking at them," he said, "and of their quality or even number I remained ignorant; they were simply in the way." Nevertheless, to allow these works of art, the "light of the country," to depart for foreign lands must have seemed to him like amputating and selling a piece of Japan itself. When he advocated for openness to Western civilization during the age of upheaval that was the Meiji period, it was not because he wanted to make Japan a replica of the countries of the West. Rather, it was because he had seen Japan's Asian neighbors fall to Great Power imperialism one after another, and believed that Westernization was the path Japan must take if it was to avoid colonization and remain an independent country in its original form. And the foundation of that original form—the guarantee of Japanese identity—was art.

Fukuzawa's bulk purchase of the artworks meant for export is thought to have taken place in 1881 or 1882. This was around the same time that he published an essay that cannot be overlooked if his thinking is to be understood: "On the Imperial Household" (Teishitsuron), published in twelve installments between April and May 1882 on the editorial page of his newspaper *Current Events* (*Jiji shinpō*). In this work, Fukuzawa argued that the Imperial household's role was not to exercise direct rule but rather to "stand outside political society" and be a spiritual comfort and psychological support to the nation's people as a whole—"to be a center of refined learning, and to preserve the arts and rescue them from decline," thus taking on once more their historic role as patrons of arts and letters. (In the case of the arts, Fukuzawa's wish was granted eight years later when the Imperial Household Artist system was established in 1890.)

"The arts" for whose "preserv[ation]" Fukuzawa argued in the essay were "the arts unique to Japan," cultivated over the nation's long history. Fukuzawa goes further, also calling them "Japan's unique civilization"— nothing other than the "light of the country." The specific list of arts that the observant and practical Fukuzawa offers is characteristically broad: calligraphy, sculpture, and crafts (*maki-e* lacquerware, woven and dyed textiles, pottery, metalwork, and swordsmithing), of course, but also music, Noh theater, *ikebana* flower arranging, the tea ceremony, and the use of fragrances. Fukuzawa also includes "the various schools of etiquette" along with the martial arts—of the sword, the spear, horse riding, archery, judo, sumo, and swimming—as well as carpentry, plastering, *bonsai*, landscaping, cookery, and even the board games of *go* and *shōgi*. In what we today would call the culture of everyday life, Fukuzawa located the core of Japanese identity.

This was not the first time Fukuzawa had argued that the state had an important role to play as protector of the nation's cultural heritage. As early as May 1878, he contributed an article entitled "On the Adornments of the Nation" (Kuni no sōshoku no koto) to the *Journal of the People* (*Minkan zasshi*) in which he strongly criticized the anti-Buddhist atmosphere current at the time—symbolized by the popular slogan *haibutsu kishaku*, or "discard Buddhism, destroy the Buddha"—and lamented that so many superb examples of Buddhist architecture were being allowed to rot away. The state, he argued, must step in.

Fukuzawa's attitude towards cultural preservation must have been based in large part on his early experiences on information-gathering expeditions to the West, particularly the shogunate's 1862 embassy to Europe when Fukuzawa was 29. The embassy visited France, England, Holland, Prussia, Russia, and Portugal, and Fukuzawa diligently studied the institutions and systems of governance, society, military affairs, and manufacturing they encountered. But he also made time to visit the British Museum, along with many other museums and galleries. He visited the Great London Exposition, which happened to coincide with the embassy's stay, and even made a pilgrimage to South London to see the Crystal Palace constructed for the 1851 Great Exhibition and then moved out of the city once the event was over.

Seeing the way each country carefully preserved the priceless artistic heritage born of its history, Fukuzawa surely sensed the paean to national love and pride this represented, as well as the possibility of using such heritage as a foundation for national independence and glory. Although often seen as a leader in the destruction of old institutions and an advocate of rapid Westernization, when it came to the arts Fukuzawa was a true traditionalist who never lost his love of or respect for history.

(2009)

Blossoms of Devotion:
Goshun, Buson, and the White Plum

Early in the summer of 2008, the Miho Museum near Shigaraki in Shiga Prefecture held an exhibition centered around the late eighteenth-century haiku poet and painter Yosa Buson. One of the items on display was a small wooden statue of Buson himself, kneeling upright in *seiza* position wearing a cap and *haori* jacket. The statue's gaze was directed straight ahead, but to judge from the inkstone on its knee and the hand reaching toward it, it depicted Buson in the act of mulling over ideas for a haiku to write on the fan open in his other hand.

There are many images of Buson, including self-portraits, but wooden statues are rare. Written on the front of the statue's base was *Buson-ō*, naming the subject with a respectful form of address for older men, and at the back was a longer message: "Tenmei 3 [1784], year of the Water Rabbit, twelfth month, twenty-fifth day/Aged sixty-eight/Inspired by a portrait at the age of sixty/After purification and ablution/Made by Gekkei." (In fact, most of Tenmei 3 corresponds to 1783 in the Western calendar, but the solar and lunar New Year do not line up exactly, and Buson actually died in early 1784.) In other words, the statue was made in remembrance of Buson shortly after he passed away, based on a portrait from when he was sixty years old—an important milestone in Japan, known as *kanreki* or "circling the calendar," since the Chinese sequence of years repeats in a sixty-year cycle. Gekkei was an apprentice of Buson's in both painting and haiku and was present at his teacher's death. And not merely present— Gekkei was entrusted with the task of conveying Buson's last poems to the world. All evidence suggests that Buson considered Gekkei one of his clos-est and most trustworthy companions.

Buson died in the early hours of the morning on the twenty-fifth day of the twelfth month of Tenmei 3 (January 17, 1784, by the Western cal-endar), just as the obituary on the statue's base says. The details of his final hours are recorded in "Record of Elder Yahan's End" (Yahan-ō shūenki), "Yahan" being Buson's haiku pen name. The "Record" was written by Takai Kitō, another of Buson's haiku apprentices, and included at the be-ginning of the posthumous memorial anthology *The Juniper* (*Karahiba*).

According to Kitō, Buson's illness became grave around the middle of the twelfth month. His wife and daughter remained at his bedside night and day, and Gekkei did the same. On the twenty-fourth day of the month, Buson seemed to recover somewhat. Speaking quite normally, he called for Gekkei to write down the haiku that had come to him during his illness. By the time Gekkei had gathered together ink, brush, and pa-per, Buson had already recited two haiku:

fuyu-uguisu	winter warbler—
mukashi Ō I ga	long ago, Wang
kakine ka na	Wei's hedge
uguisu ya	warbler, why
nani gosotsukasu	are you rustling?—
yabu no shimo	the frost on the grove

He still seemed to be thinking, however, and eventually he recited a third poem, which he instructed Gekkei to give the title "Early spring":

shiraume ni	to white plum blossoms
akaru yo bakari to	the night has just begun
narinikeri	to dawn

"Making these three poems the last he spoke in life," Kitō writes, "he stilled his mind for his passing as if asleep and joyously crossed over [to the Pure Land]." The white plum haiku became Buson's death poem. In the final moments of his life, having cut away all worldly thoughts, did his fading consciousness dream of white plum blossoms standing resolute in the cool air of daybreak as the air of dawn crept in? The crisp, clear imagery, redolent of some translucent fragrance, leaves an indelible impression as the final world at which Buson—also a master painter—arrived.

To Gekkei, who had carefully written down his teacher's death poem as he fought back his tears, that impression was surely even stronger. From that point on, white plum blossom imagery must have been inextricably entangled with his feelings regarding his deceased teacher.

After he dictated these final haiku to Gekkei, Buson is said to have closed his eyes and asked "Is the night still deep?" He had already lost his sense of the actual time. Gekkei's response was a haiku delivered through tears:

ake muttsu to	the sixth hour of morning
hoete kōru ya	howls and freezes
kane no koe	the voice of the bell

"Howls and freezes" is fierce language that gives insight into the bitter grief that Gekkei could not suppress. No doubt this same grief was what later drove him to carve a portrait of his teacher as he was in life.

Matsumura Gekkei was born to the household of an official at the gold mint in Kyoto. He is said to have shown talent for painting and poetry from a young age. He apprenticed himself to Buson chiefly to learn haiku, but he also absorbed Buson's richly atmospheric style of "literati painting" (*bunjinga*). In fact, it seems that from around this time he had more recognition as a painter than as a haiku poet. Certainly it was Kitō and not Gekkei who became the third master of the Yahantei school. (Buson had been the second, inheriting the title and the school from his own teacher Hayano Hajin.) "Gekkei" was actually Matsumura's haiku name, but today he is better known by his art name "Goshun," and this is what will be used for the rest of the article.

After Buson's death, Goshun was accepted an apprentice of the painter Maruyama Ōkyo, one of Buson's friends, whose naturalistic style was very different from Buson's literati paintings. Goshun even participated alongside Ōkyo's other apprentices in a project to paint the sliding doors at

Goshun, *White Plum Blossoms* (*Hakubai-zu byōbu*), Edo period (ca. 1789–1801). Itsuō Art Museum.

Daijōji Temple. But Ōkyo always treated Goshun more as Buson's leading disciple than his own apprentice. Indeed, right up until Ōkyo's death in 1795, *he* was the true apprentice, absorbing everything about Goshun's style and making it his own.

Most art histories teach that after Ōkyo's death, Goshun's unique artistic style, in which intricate depiction of the subject was combined with elegant touches of emotion, formed the foundation for the Kyoto Shijō school. This is essentially true, but it does not mean that Goshun simply abandoned literati painting and shifted to naturalism after Buson's death. Even while studying under Ōkyo, the lessons of his departed teacher and the experience of being present at his death lived on within Goshun, and cannot but have exerted an influence on his later creative endeavors.

I was encouraged to explore this idea by Goshun's great work *White Plum Blossoms*, a pair of six-panel folding screens held by the Itsuō Art Museum in Ikeda, Osaka Prefecture. One of Goshun's most famous works and an Important Cultural Property, the work depicts plum trees drawn on a field of calm blue. On the right is a single white-blossomed tree with one startlingly angled branch; on the left, two more trees stretch out their branches to the right as if yearning for the first. The skillful composition and cool lyricism of this masterpiece give it the air of a peaceful night

somehow beyond the everyday. It leaves a deep impression on the viewer; no one who sees it even once is likely to forget it. Note, too, that the night depicted is not entirely pitch-black. As far as can be determined from the paintings themselves, it is just bright enough to sense the whiteness of the plum blossoms.

The blue field is a unique element, without parallel in similar work. It was not painted on; Goshun reportedly had raw silk thread dyed with indigo and then woven into a plain-weave fabric that was pasted onto the screens. The effort that must have been required reveals the depth of Goshun's feeling regarding this work.

The circumstances of the creation of *White Plum Blossoms* are not known. Goshun "signed" the screens with the cursive seal he had only used in the 1780s, and the brushwork on the plum trees already shows a move towards the style of Ōkyo's Maruyama school. From this it has been concluded that the work was painted in the late 1780s or early 1790s, but it seems to me we can narrow down the year of its creation even further.

Plum blossoms shining palely in the night—this is precisely the world of Buson's death poem. While creating this work, the memory of recording his teacher's final poem himself surely rose within Goshun's heart. But what if we were more daring and imagined that it was the other way around—that Buson's white plum blossom poem inspired Goshun's unique creation?

The idea is quite convincing if we imagine that the work was produced in early 1790. This corresponds to the twelfth month of Kansei 1, when the ceremony was held for the sixth anniversary of Buson's death. Perhaps *White Plum Blossoms* was a memorial work for his departed teacher.

Indeed, much later, on the 24th anniversary of Buson's death (early 1808, by the Western calendar), Goshun was still dutifully making ceremonial offerings. It seems that his devotion to his old teacher remained vital in his heart throughout his entire life.

(2010)

Dragons, Tigers, and Museums

Among the commemorative stamp designs selected for Japan's Philately Week issue in 2010 was the *Dragon and Tiger* set of folding screens by Hashimoto Gahō, a painter of the Meiji period. Hashimoto's imposing work was selected, of course, because 2010 was the Year of the Dragon according to the Chinese zodiac.

Of the twelve animals of the Chinese zodiac—excluding the dragon, which as a mythical beast is in a separate class entirely—virtually all are familiar, everyday presences to the Japanese. The tiger is the exception: Japan has never been part of its natural habitat. Even so, the Japanese have been familiar with the animal since ancient times due to its prominence in Chinese culture, including the zodiac, the "Four Gods" cosmology (in which four animal deities are held to control the cardinal directions and seasons), folklore (*koji*), and Buddhist morality tales (*setsuwa*).

As such, Japanese art has not lacked for depictions of tigers, from the charming example in Kōsanji Temple's *Frolicking Animals* (*Chōjū giga*) scrolls to the work of countless painters of the Edo period willing to try their hand at depicting this fierce beast that they had never seen—not least Maruyama Ōkyo, who was sometimes called the "painter of tigers."

The earliest tiger motifs in Japanese art history can be found on silver pots and mirrors among the ancient treasures of the Shōsoin, but the earliest surviving pictures of tigers by a Japanese artist are probably the wall paintings in Kitora Tomb and Takamatsuzuka Tomb, which are thought to date from the late seventh or early eighth century. The White Tiger of Kitora Tomb in particular made headlines in recent years when it was captured on camera for the first time.

Along with the Azure Dragon, the Vermillion Bird, and the Black Tortoise, this White Tiger is one of the Four Gods mentioned above. Each of these divine animals is linked to a different season, cardinal direction, and color, and the whole combines into a coherent model of the world. The tiger's season is autumn, its direction is west, and its color is, of course, white. (As for the other animals, the Azure Dragon is linked to spring and the east, the Vermillion Bird to summer and the south, and the Black Tortoise to winter and the north.) The echoes of this philosophy can be seen in the colored tassels at the corners of the sumo ring in Ryōgoku Sumo Hall. When I was a child, these were not tassels but pillars. Each was a different color—red, blue, white, and black, naturally—and the radio commentators would say things like "He's ferociously pushing him towards the white pillar." In representing the Four Gods, these pillars (or tassels) make the sumo ring a world unto itself.

To ancient urbanites, the Four Gods were also protective deities, and old capitals like Heijō- and Heian-kyō were laid out according to these ideas. The imperial order for the construction of the Heijō-kyō palace, dated 710, observes that "the geography of Heijō is in accord with the Four Gods layout, and the three mountains will anchor and pacify the whole." The formula for the ideal city in Four Gods philosophy was very specific: mountains to the north, a river to the east, a body of water to the south, and a road to the west. As a result, the tiger had the important task of protecting the town at its entrance, where it met the western road. Edo, which was modeled on Heian-kyō, inherited these ideas (albeit with axial lines somewhat skewed by the exigencies of geography), and a "Gate of the White Tiger" was erected where the city connected with the Tōkaidō road to the west. That gate is gone now, but the area still bears the name "Toranomon," meaning "tiger gate."

Compared to the Four Gods, the twelve animals of the Chinese zodiac are much more deeply embedded in everyday life in Japan. Every New Year, Japanese households send out countless postcards to family and friends, more often than not featuring an image of that year's animal. The zodiac animals have appeared in many forms throughout the history of Japanese art.

At a special exhibition held in 2010 at the Mitsubishi Ichigōkan Museum of Art entitled *From Dream to Reality: The Iwasaki/Mitsubishi Collection*, three paintings from Meiji painter Yamamoto Hōsui's Chinese zodiac series were on display. This series is one of Hōsui's most famous achievements and of great importance to the history of Western-style art in the Meiji period. It is also highly unique, even anomalous, as a pictorial representation of the zodiac animals. In most works on this theme, animals—naturally—play the starring role. Hōsui's tableaus, however, place humans at the center, depicting scenes from history, legend, or simply everyday life. For example, the zodiac painting corresponding to the cow or ox is called *Altair* (*Kengyūsei*—literally "cowherd star") and takes as its theme the legend of Tanabata, in which the weaver (Vega) and the cowherd (Altair) are separated by the Milky Way and can meet for just one night each year. The painting is dominated by Hōsui's depiction of Vega, who reclines in dazzling finery. Altair, on the other hand, is in the far distance, barely even visible. Elegant and alluring as this work is, it falls naturally into the genre of *bijinga*, "pictures of beautiful women."

An interesting tale is told about how Hōsui came to paint his Chinese zodiac series. The story begins with Yanosuke, then head of the house of Iwasaki, requesting that Hōsui paint a picture with a rabbit motif for his son, Koyata, who had been born in that year. Hōsui complied, presenting Yanosuke with a picture of two rabbits frolicking in a meadow. Pleased with this result, Yanosuke next asked Hōsui to paint a *bijinga*. Hōsui fulfilled the commission with a tableau that happened to include a *fusuma-e* of a dragon—or perhaps the dragon was a carefully calculated addition. In either case, Hōsui pointed out that, placed side-by-side, the two paintings corresponded to two of the twelve Chinese zodiac animals, and proposed to complete the series. Yanosuke loved the idea, promising to buy the series when it was done and put it on display in his mansion.

The tiger painting in the series is based on a legend involving Odai no Kata, mother of the first Edo shogun Tokugawa Ieyasu. After visiting Hōraiji Temple and praying to Bhaiṣajyaguru (known in Japanese as Yakushi Nyorai or "Medicine Buddha"), the legend goes, she was visited in a dream by the one of his Twelve Heavenly Generals, a tiger deity, who entered the breast of her garment; when she woke, she was pregnant with Ieyasu. Hōsui's depiction of the scene has a phantasmagorical atmosphere, with Odai no Kata sleeping soundly as the ghostly tiger appears above her breast. Each of the paintings in the series has its own distinct mood in this way—a testament to Hōsui's excellent imagination. The first two paintings in the series, corresponding to the hare and the dragon, were somehow lost, but Mitsubishi Heavy Industries owns the remaining ten and keeps them on display at the Senshōkaku mansion in Nagasaki. (For the sake of completeness, allow me to mention that Yanosuke was also the original owner of Hashimoto Gahō's *Dragon and Tiger* folding screens.)

One more story about museums, dragons, and tigers:

The Ōhara Museum of Art in Kurashiki, Okayama Prefecture, was established in 1930 as the first permanent museum in Japan dedicated to modern Western art. The museum stands at the center of Kurashiki's Bikan Historical Quarter, in which the streetscape of the Edo period is still largely preserved, overlooking the Kurashiki River with its calmly swimming swans. Just across the bridge is Ōhara House, a nationally designated Important Cultural Property, alongside Yūrinsō Villa, which has attracted notice from historians of modern architecture as a residence combining Japanese and Western ideas and techniques. Few visitors to the town no-

Hashimoto Gahō, *Dragon and Tiger* (*Ryūko-zu byōbu*), 1895. Seikadō Bunko Art Museum.

tice, but the railings of the stone bridge across the river are actually carved with a large dragon motif, as are the *ranma* (transoms) at Yūrinsō Villa.

Together, these dragons seem to stand quiet watch over the town and its museum. Both were designed by the painter Kojima Torajirō. Torajirō was a close friend and collaborator of Ōhara Magosaburō, founder of the Ōhara Museum. Regarding the museum in particular, it might be more accurate to call him Magosaburō's partner. It was Torajirō's urgent desire to make European artwork accessible to Japanese painters that inspired Magosaburō to take the first steps towards creating a museum for that purpose. Because Magosaburō's own tastes originally leaned more towards Japanese and Asian antiquities, though, he left the selection of works for the museum entirely in Torajirō's hands. Torajirō repaid this trust by calling repeatedly on painters like Monet and Matisse in their studios, visiting countless exhibitions and galleries, and generally sparing no effort to gather only the most superior works. The collection he assembled is highly regarded around the world even today.

As well as being the 80th anniversary of the Ōhara Museum of Art's founding, 2010 was also the 130th anniversary of Magosaburō's birth. To commemorate the occasion, the museum held a special exhibition that autumn entitled *Ōhara Magosaburō: Views of Japanese Art*. Some of the works on display belonged to the museum, but all were originally in Magosaburō's

personal collection. As well as two designated National Treasures—*Landscape* (*Sansui-zu*) by Sesshū, and *Court Lady* (*Kyūjo-zu*), attributed to the Chinese painter Qian Xuan—there were works by Aoki Mokubei, Maruyama Ōkyo, Okada Beisanjin, and other painters, largely of the Edo period. Tigers and dragons were represented by Ōkyo's *Sitting Tiger* (*Mōko-zu*) and Nagasawa Rosetsu's powerful *Dragons* (*Gunryū-zu*). The exhibition was both homage to Magosaburō and manifesto for the future direction of the museum.

Incidentally, the reason Torajirō employed the dragon motif in particular in the ornamental details of the museum's architecture was because Magosaburō was born in that year. For Torajirō, the dragon was a symbol of his close friend and patron. Given that his own name included the word for "tiger" (*tora*) we might say that it was a close collaboration between tiger and dragon that made the establishment of this superb museum possible.

(2010)

Interpretation as Transformation

Guillaume Apollinaire is perhaps best known today as the lyricist of the popular chanson "Mirabeau Bridge" (Le Pont Mirabeau), but Apollinaire loved the new and avant-garde above all. His own oeuvre includes a book of poetry entitled *Calligrammes*, in which words are arranged into pictures on the page. "It's Raining" (Il pleut) has long lines that run diagonally down the page like falling rain; in the latter half of "The Stabbed Dove and the Fountain" (La Colombe poignardée et le jet d'eau), the words dance like a fountain's spray. He also wrote many fantastical short stories, some of which would be considered science fiction today.

Apollinaire was a prolific critic as well. He had substantial influence in the art world and actively supported avant-garde movements that enjoyed little popularity at the time, from Picasso's Cubism to Robert Delaunay's Orphism, the latter of which he even named. Within the artistic circles of Paris, Apollinaire was a rather impish *provocateur*.

Nor was he any less dynamic in private life. When the First World War broke out, Apollinaire promptly volunteered for military service and, later, to fight at the front. But he was not there long before he was shot in the head and escorted back to safety, eventually undergoing three rounds of open-brain surgery. The seriousness of his injury is clear from a photo taken of Apollinaire in his army uniform with his head wrapped up in white bandages. (Picasso also sketched Apollinaire in this state.)

Despite his ordeal, which must have left him quite weak physically, Apollinaire remained in high spirits and continued to make appearances at events in the Parisian art world. His bandaged head left a strong impression on people, and his image as a patriotic hero proved unexpectedly useful at the scandalous debut of *Parade* in May 1917, while the war was still ongoing.

Performed by the Ballets Russes under Sergei Diaghilev, *Parade* was a razor-sharp work of avant-garde theater by an all-star lineup of fearless young artists. Jean Cocteau wrote the libretto, Erik Satie the music, costumes and set design were by Picasso, and Léonide Massine was the choreographer. The work was designed expressly to irritate the sensibilities of the average theatergoer, and the booing began almost as soon as the curtains opened. Before long the abuse and invective hurled by both audience and performers threatened to escalate into an all-out brawl. But, reports say, when Apollinaire rose to appeal for calm, the sight of the injured critic so moved those present that the crisis was averted.

Apollinaire himself was of course on the avant-garde side of the dispute. In fact, he had even written a short piece for the program in which he described the world of *Parade* as *"une sorte de sur-réalisme."* The word *surréalisme*, with the intended meaning "super-realism," was thus one of the many coined by Apollinaire himself. He must have been quite taken with his invention, because he deployed it again (without the hyphen) in the preface to his verse play *The Breasts of Tiresias* (*Les Mamelles de Tirésias*), describing the work as a *"drame surréaliste."* Thus, while Surrealism as a school may have begun with André Breton's *Manifeste du surréalisme* of 1924, this hugely important twentieth-century movement owes its name to Apollinaire. (And, of course, as a fellow poet, Breton was close to Apollinaire too.)

In fact, the connection between Apollinaire and Surrealism goes beyond the movement's name. Surrealism's new contributions to artistic expression were many, but its widening of the possibilities of interpretation was among the most important. Before Surrealism, interpreting a work of art was held to consist in correctly understanding the intentions of the artist in creating it—that is, in accurately receiving the message sent by the work's creator. If the viewer misunderstood the artist's intentions or "received" a message that the artist had not sent, their interpretation of the work would be incorrect.

This view is obviously premised on the idea that behind every work lies a definite, if possibly obscure, message from its creator. What is required of the audience or recipient of the work is, along with an analysis of the work itself, a correct reading of its message. This reading must be based on contemporary documentation, the actual words of the artist, and similar materials: no other form of interpretation is permitted.

But there are works that have no clear message—which are completed only by the interpretations of their audience. The audience in this case does not passively receive a one-way message but rather participates to a certain extent in the act of creation. Umberto Eco pointed out how common works of this sort had become in the twentieth century. "Open works" (*opere aperte*), as he called them, are finally complete only when interpretation is added to the intentions of their creator. For musical works, this interpretation comes from performers or listeners; for paintings, from viewers. Surrealists often used mysterious, incomprehensible imagery to appeal to the viewer's imagination, a practice strongly influenced by the work of Giorgio de Chirico. The Surrealists were fascinated by Chirico's mystic tableaus; at André Breton's Bureau of Surrealistic Research, there was reportedly always something by Chirico on the wall. One painting that particularly stimulated the imagination of the Surrealists was Chirico's *Portrait de Guillaume Apollinaire*.

The *Portrait* is considered one of the best examples of Chirico's "metaphysical art" (*pittura metafisica*) and happened to be on display at the National Art Center, Tokyo's special exhibition *Le Surréalisme* as I wrote these lines in 2011. But its label at the exhibition identifies it as *Portrait prémonitoire de Guillaume Apollinaire*: the portrait has become "premonitory." This rather ostentatious new title reflects a later reinterpretation of the work by the Surrealists.

The foreground of the *Portrait* contains motifs that often appeared in Chirico's work in that period—the head and shoulders of a marble statue in dark glasses, fish and shell molds—while Apollinaire's profile can be seen in a space opened like a window at the rear of the tableau. Silhouetted against a field of dark green, the poet could almost be a ghost, but what is mysterious is the white circle drawn on his head right where he would later be wounded. After Apollinaire was shot, the painting came to be seen as having predicted his fate in a reinterpretation that spread from viewer to

Giorgio de Chirico, *Premonitory Portrait of Guillaume Apollinaire* (*Portrait prémonitoire de Guillaume Apollinaire*), 1914. Centre Georges Pompidou.

viewer. The idea was, of course, nothing but a myth that appealed to Surrealist tastes—put bluntly, a fiction—but it undeniably heightened the mystic atmosphere around the work.

Even Chirico himself accepted the new interpretation. In a magazine obituary for the poet written years later, he recalled gathering in Apollinaire's study to exchange arguments with like-minded fellows, adding:

> Several of my metaphysical works ended up on the walls of that study, including one in which I had depicted him like a target in a shooting gallery. It later seemed to me that I had foretold his head injury.

The *Portrait* is thus a rare example of a work that came to transcend the original intentions of its creator and take on a different meaning altogether.

By "rare," of course, I mean in the context of the West. If the reader will forgive the leap, in Japan such cases are not necessarily rare at all. Works of art in the West are ultimately produced by individuals; accordingly, the idea that interpreting art consists in correctly understanding its creator's intentions remains strong today. But consider, for example, Japanese linked verse forms like *renga* and *renku*. Creators in these genres do not simply accept the lines produced by other participants. Instead, they must use the contributions of others as a starting point for depicting a new and different world. The result might be called a chain of reinterpretation.

Similar results are possible even for a poem that stands alone. For example, one of Bashō's disciples once brought his master the following haiku for critique:

iwahana ya	the outcropping rock—
koko ni mo hitori	here, too, another
tsuki no kyaku	guest of the moon

The student explained that he had made his way one night to a flat outcrop he suspected would be ideal for moon-viewing only to find someone else already there. Hearing this, Bashō suggested that the poem would be even better if "another guest of the moon" referred to the poet himself, announcing that he had once more ventured out alone, rather than someone already at the outcrop. A new interpretation can make all the difference.

(2011)

Interpretation as Creative Act

A reader of the previous essay, "Interpretation as Transformation," wrote to ask which student of Bashō wrote the "outcropping rock" haiku and where the account of their conversation might be found. The poet was Mukai Kyorai, traditionally considered one of Bashō's ten most important disciples, and the account is from *Kyorai's Recollections of Bashō* (*Kyorai shō*).

To recap, the *Recollections* has Kyorai explaining to Bashō that the haiku depicted the moment of discovering someone on a rocky outcrop already enjoying the moon. In response, Bashō says:

> How much more poetic (*fūryū*) it would be if "here, too, another guest of the moon" were simply you announcing your own arrival! You ought to make the work one of self-announcement alone.

Reflecting on this later, Kyorai writes:

> As a work of self-announcement, the work invokes the image of a true poet and becomes ten times better than it was. Truly, the author of this poem did not know its heart.

Many such episodes shedding light on Bashō's thinking can be found in Kyorai's *Recollections*. Consider the discussion of this celebrated haiku by Nozawa Bonchō:

shimogyō ya	downtown Kyoto—
yuki tsumu ue ni	atop the fallen snow
yoru no ame	the night's rain

The last two lines of this haiku were completed first, followed by a group discussion of what should come before them. Bashō declared that the first line *must* be "downtown Kyoto." When Bonchō seemed unconvinced, Bashō insisted that if anyone could find a better solution, he would never argue haiku poetics again.

It was common, in that period, for haiku poets to exchange opinions and arguments with other members of their circle as they worked. According to Kagami Shikō's *The Pine Grove with Kudzu* (*Kuzu no matsubara*), for example, Bashō came up with the last two lines of his famous "old pond" haiku first—"frog jumps in / sound of water"—and was considering what the first line should be when his disciple Kikaku suggested "*yamabuki ya,*" "a kerria." This colorful proposal is typical of Kikaku, whose tastes ran somewhat to the gaudy, and the finished haiku—"a kerria / frog jumps in / sound of water" would not have been a bad one, redolent in its way of a certain languid, late spring elegance. Nevertheless, Bashō rejected Kikaku's idea in favor of the well-known "old pond," which Shikō describes as a case of discarding the florid (*hanayakasa*) in favor of the concrete (*jitsu*).

But if so, what is this "concrete" Shikō speaks of? It clearly cannot refer to something actually seen, as the image of the "old pond" is not an everyday one. On the contrary, the phrase evokes in the mind's eye a still pool shrouded in eternal silence within a remote, forgotten grove. A single frog leaps into the water, and for a moment the air rings with that faint sound before silence descends on the scene once more. After the brief disturbance, the silence is all the heavier, the world all the more remote, and this is surely the world Bashō intended. It approaches the same poetic territory as this line by the Chinese poet Wang Ji of the Northern and Southern Dynasties era (420–589):

鳥鳴山更幽　　　a bird cries—the mountain is quieter still

On the other hand, Bashō's haiku can also be interpreted as a much more everyday scene. Frogs are sociable by nature; walking a footpath between rice fields at dusk in early spring, the chorus from both sides is almost deafening. And if one frog leaps into the water, the others follow one by one. The "sound of water" in this interpretation is lively and vigorous rather than quiet and remote. In fact, there is a haiku on this theme by Mikami Wakyū, a contemporary of Bashō's from Kyoto:

hitotsu tobu	one jumps
oto ni mina tobu	at the sound, they all jump—
kaeru kana	frogs

Indeed, that many commentaries explicitly argue that the *kaeru* of Bashō's haiku must be read as a single frog only confirms that the plural interpretation is in fact possible.

The frog's solitude or lack thereof is actually a more pressing question for non-Japanese readers, because in English, French, and the other languages of Western Europe, nouns *must* be either singular or plural. One survey of around thirty English translations of the "old pond" haiku found that while most had the frog in the singular, there were a few exceptions. In fact, one of the translations with multiple frogs was by Lafcadio Hearn, who was of course resident in Japan and well acquainted with the country:

Old pond — frogs jumped in — sound of water.

It is interesting to consider what sort of scene the poem must have conjured up for Hearn, given his first-hand experience of nineteenth-century Japan.

A similar debate arose at an international symposium at the Centre Georges Pompidou in Paris attended by Japanese and French scholars, myself among their number. The debate began when another haiku by Bashō was mentioned. Note the underlined part below:

kare-eda ni	on a withered branch
karasu no tomarikeri	a crow/crows come to rest
aki no kure	autumn evening

One of the French attendees asked whether the crow was singular or plural. Someone from the Japanese side replied that since the object of the haiku was to convey a sense of deep desolation through the image of a lone, forlorn crow alighting on a bough as the autumn sun set, it could only be singular. But then the Japanese poet and critic Ōoka Makoto rose to his feet and reported that there existed a copy of this haiku known to be in Bashō's own hand, and the picture accompanying it showed many crows on the branch. If, as this picture suggested, the haiku was supposed to invoke multiple crows against the setting sun, its interpretation would change dramatically.

One of the innovations of the "old pond" haiku was the frog's leap into the water; until then, frogs had largely appeared in poetry for their voice. The same thing could be said of the crows in the "withered branch" haiku. The term "autumn evening" brings to mind first of all the crows in Sei Shōnagon's *Pillow Book* (see p. 176) that "return to their roosts in threes and fours, twos and threes, and even their hurried flight is moving." In noticing that Bashō takes these scattered birds and sets them down on a branch, we catch a glimpse of his poetic technique.

I do not mean to imply by any of this that the multiple-crow interpretation is after all the only permissible one. If a reader sees only one crow in their mind's eye, and shares in the deep desolation of the image, Bashō would surely be satisfied with that, too. There is not necessarily a single correct answer.

That may seem a rather unhelpful attitude for a creator to adopt, but it makes sense if we recall that Bashō was a true haiku poet. Haiku originally evolved from *hokku*, literally the "opening verse" of a collaborative form called *renku*, "linked verse." Once the *hokku* was provided, the next participant augmented it with a *wakiku* ("accompanying verse"), a two-line segment with the role of fixing an interpretation of the *hokku*. As a result, the *hokku* could not be too conclusive; to be sufficiently "open" to the *wakiku*, it had to permit a diversity of interpretations.

This does not mean, of course, that any interpretation at all was permitted. As participants forge the chain of *renku*, each succeeding link breathes new life into the previous one even as it opens a new world for the next. The question of how to interpret the preceding verse and then pivot from that to a new world was precisely where the art lay. In that sense, each verse in a *renku* sequence is a poetic act that combines interpretation *and* creation. Similarly, in his comments on Kyorai's "outcropping rock" haiku, Bashō revealed a new form for the work that had not occurred even to its author—another case of interpretation as a creative act.

(2011)

Bridges and the Japanese

Outside Paris—quite a long way outside Paris, truth be told—lies the commune of Giverny, best known for the retreat in which Impressionist master Claude Monet spent his final years. Monet's residence and gardens have been kept just as they was during his life and still attract sightseers today.

Along with a riot of colorful flowers, the gardens contain a pond fed by a stream diverted from a nearby river. This pond is where Monet cultivated the water lilies he painted like a man possessed in his later years, making it highly popular with tourists. To visitors from Japan such as myself, however, the Japanese-style arched bridge over the pond is of even greater interest. Monet greatly admired Japanese art, amassing a considerable personal collection of ukiyo-e prints over the course of his life, and the bridge is a sort of homage to Japan.

Of course, Monet never visited Japan himself. His "Japanese tastes" were cultivated chiefly through ukiyo-e and other artworks, and the arched bridge derives from the same source. We have many paintings by Monet of his garden with the bridge at the center of the tableau like a great rainbow, and all of them are more or less identical in composition to Hiroshige's "Inside Kameido Tenjin Shrine" (Kameido Tenjin keidai) from *One Hundred Famous Views of Edo* (*Meisho Edo hyakkei*). The bridge was clearly Monet's attempt to recreate in his own gardens the Japan he had come to know through ukiyo-e. But there is one important difference. In Hiroshige's print, the arch of the bridge is so high that it almost forms a perfect semicircle, while Monet's has a much gentler slope.

The shape of Monet's bridge is, of course, much more convenient for those actually crossing it. In Giverny, many visitors enjoy strolling unhurriedly across the bridge; this would barely be possible on Hiroshige's bridge. Nor is this bridge shape unique to Hiroshige. The bridge outside Sumiyoshi Shrine, for example, which has appeared on folding screen paintings since ancient times, is depicted with an arch so steep it barely seems crossable at all. The arched bridge on the grounds of Tsurugaoka Hachimangū Shrine in Kamakura is similar. Japanese bridges of this sort simply are not made to be easily crossable by humans. If anything, they appear to reject passage rather than facilitate it.

Bridges not only connect two worlds, they also form a boundary between them. To the Japanese, these arched bridges were placed at the entrances of shrines precisely in order to divide the human world from the world of the gods. Even regular bridges seem to have carried a strong suggestion that the other bank of the river was another world. To cross the bridge was to set out on a journey to that world. The ancient Tōkaidō road ran from Nihonbashi in Edo to Sanjō Ōhashi in Kyoto—two bridges, as the *hashi* or *bashi* element in their names indicates. This is no coincidence.

By "another world" I mean a dimension beyond the everyday world we know. In Japanese legend, bridges are often places where strange figures are met, hinting at their role as entrances to other worlds. The famous "catalog of bridges" (*hashi-zukushi*) at the climax of Chikamatsu Monzaemon's *jōruri* puppet play *The Love Suicides at Amijima* (*Shinjū ten no Amijima*) also reflects this view. The journey of Koharu and Jihei across the bridges gradually becomes a journey to the land of the dead, and the final bridge becomes the boundary between life and death itself.

This view of bridges as both boundary of and entrance to another world seems to linger within the Japanese sensibility even today, as in, for example, Yoshimoto Banana's short story called "Moonlight Shadow." Written before her breakthrough hit *Kitchen*, "Moonlight Shadow" is a tale of great pathos about a girl who has lost her lover in an accident and jogs every morning in an attempt to overcome her sadness. One day, following the directions of a mysterious woman she met while jogging, she goes to the foot of a bridge at dawn (the boundary between night and day). This was the place where she and her lover always parted after spending time together. There, for just a few moments, the girl sees the gently smiling form of her lover swathed in mist on the far bank of the river. She cannot approach or speak to him, however, and eventually, with a final wave, he disappears into the mists. The symbolic meaning of the bridge as boundary here is clear.

If bridges are imbued with this powerful symbolism in the Japanese sensibility, this should be readily visible not only in art and literature but in a wider range of domains of expression as well. And indeed, bridges often feature as a meeting and parting place in popular songs. Moritaka Chisato's "Watarase Bridge" (Watarasebashi), for example, expresses the sadness of separation from a lover who was fond of watching the sun set from the titular bridge. This is just one of many examples. I explored this motif further in a special feature written with a friend for a magazine named *Japanese Aesthetics* (*Nihon no bigaku*) in 1998.

(1998)

The Glittering Vague

In 2014, the National Museum of Modern Art in Kitanomaru Park, Tokyo, held the first major Hishida Shunsō retrospective for some time. I am known for having voiced the rather brash opinion that if we had only the work of the Japan Art Institute (Nippon Bijutsuin), we would need no other Japanese-style painting from the Meiji period; if we had only Hishida Shunsō, we would need no other member of the Institute; and if we had only Shunsō's *Fallen Leaves* (*Ochiba*), we would need no more of his work. Today, however, surveying Shunsō's accomplishments as a painter in his 36 short years of life, he seems to me a genius whose work had an enormous, indelible effect on not only on the art of the Meiji period, but also on modern Japanese painting more generally—indeed, the whole history of Japanese art.

Shunsō secures a place for himself in this history through his successful exploration of fresh forms of expression for a new age while still maintaining the traditions of the past. Put bluntly, his work was a reformation of Japanese-style painting itself. Like most reformations, it aroused both shock and opposition, attracting criticism and even ridicule from critics and journalists. The treatment of the "Vague style" (*mōrōtai*) movement promoted by Shunsō and his close friend Yokoyama Taikan, is perhaps the best example of this.

Today, the Japanese word *mōrō* still means "vague" or "indistinct," but does not necessarily have a negative connotation. This was not so, however, in Meiji Japan. Tokyo was still undergoing its rapid modernization, and one of the new menaces that had arisen were the thuggish rickshaw men who gathered around public spaces and train stations. They would lie in wait for travelers from the countryside, who they would deceive, threaten, and shake down for fees far greater than the law allowed. These men were known as *mōrō shafu*, literally "vague (or 'shady') rickshaw men," and some even joined forces to form *mōrō* unions. They were troublemakers who threatened the stability of society and unrepentantly broke social norms. In this context, it seems less of an exaggeration when Taikan says in his biography that he and Shunsō were "shunned almost like demons" for their work in the Vague style.

In terms of painterly expression, one reason Taikan and Shunsō's experiments were criticized so strongly was their rejection of the strong ink lines that had been (or had been viewed as) the vital essence of Japanese-style painting. For example, in Shunsō's 1901 work *The Farewell of Su Wu and Li Ling*, both human figures and background were criticized for being depicted in a "lineless style, entirely Western, which breaks the fundamental rules of Japanese painting technique." The term "lineless style" referred

Hishida Shunsō,
The Farewell of Su Wu and Li Ling
(*So-Ri ketsubetsu*), 1901.

to the lack of any clear outlines around the figures or on the folds of their clothing. Where Shunsō did draw outlines or clothing folds, he did so not in dark black ink but in color, and, inevitably, these "colored lines" also became a target of criticism. Even Shunsō's 1902 *Wang Zhaojun* (Ō Shōkun), which masterfully depicts the fate of the unfortunate beauty in colors both fascinating and exquisite, was criticized along these lines. Its outlines had "lost their clarity," detractors said, and it lacked expressive power as a result.

Art historians generally agree that the young members of the Japan Art Institute experimented with these bold methods in response to a request from Okakura Tenshin. Seeing the bright *pleinarisme* championed by Kuroda Seiki and becoming the mainstream in the world of Western-style art, Tenshin inquired whether Japan-style painting could not paint "light and air" as well. Indeed, looking back on the time later, Taikan wrote:

"Why not try painting the air?" he suggested. ... I started by moistening the paper, and then drew in ink on top of that. When I used a dry brush to sweep away the ink without destroying the form, I was left with a hazy atmosphere like the air on a rainy day.

Truly, this was *mōrō* itself.

But even if Tenshin did make that suggestion, his true meaning was certainly not that painters should simply recreate what they saw in nature exactly as it was. What Tenshin demanded from pictorial expression was not simple recreation of reality, but rather a kind of deep poetic sentiment born of that. He remained insistent on this point throughout his life.

In 1900, Shunsō produced a painting entitled *Tokiwazu: Princess Fuse*. The work's theme is the scene at the beginning of Takizawa Bakin's story *The Tale of Eight Dogs* (Nansō satomi hakkenden) in which Princess Fuse looks into a pond and is startled to see that her reflection has the face of a dog. The entire tableau is enveloped in a dark and gloomy atmosphere to describe which words like "vague" or "indistinct" seem eminently suitable. However, as the "Tokiwazu" (a kind of shamisen music) in the title indicates, this was originally one of Tenshin's song-inspired painting themes. In his quest for the expression of a "new Japanese-style painting," Tenshin assigned themes to the young painters of the Japan Art Institute not only from Tokiwazu but also other from genres of shamisen music, including Kiyomoto, Shinnai, and Nagauta, to make them think about what sort of painting they could make of the music.

Even in his years as the head of an art school, Tenshin had considered the assignment of themes like "boldness," "silence," and "selflessness" an important pedagogical method. Students assigned these themes were strictly forbidden from rendering them directly. If the theme was "moonlight," the moon could not appear in the painting; if it was "the sound of a flute," there could be no flute depicted. In other words, Tenshin forbade realistic expression.

Hishida Shunsō,
Tokiwazu: Princess Fuse
(*Tokiwazu: Fuse-hime*),
1900. Nagano Prefectural
Shinano Art Museum.

There is an oft-related story about Tenshin that is relevant here. He once criticized a picture of the goddess Benzaiten that Shimomura Kanzan was working on, saying that he could not hear the sound of the goddess's *biwa* from the painting. Kanzan tried changing Benzaiten's pose and made many other adjustments, but Tenshin was not satisfied. Finally, at a loss for what else to do, Kanzan added a small flower to the rock beside the goddess. "*Now* I can hear the music," said Tenshin, and his praise for the finished work was effusive.

As this episode shows, for Tenshin, paintings were not supposed to present an accurate recreation of the real world—or at least not that alone. What they needed instead was a kind of suggestiveness capable of summoning up deep emotion from within the viewer. Thus, even if he did ask the young painters of the Japan Art Institute to "paint the light and air," and even if that request was inspired by the attempts of the Impressionists to paint nature just as their senses apprehended it—in defiance of Academism—Tenshin clearly did not want Japanese-style paintings to recreate nature as it was. Indeed, Tenshin saw perceptively that even Impressionists like Monet, Sisley, and Pissarro were not simple imitators of nature. When invited to give a speech at the Saint Louis Exposition in America in 1904, he made this clear:

> [A]rt is a suggestion through nature. ... We may notice that a vast amount of conventionality exists even in the French impressionists, who are said to have given the last word of realism. Their best productions command respect, not on account of their power of painting sunlight, but in the value of the new poetry they are enabled to express through their outdoor technique.

Given the early date, this is a startlingly insightful assessment of the French Impressionists.

At around the same time, the Vague school was still being subjected to fierce criticism. Tenshin must have had the work of Taikan, Shunsō, and their fellows in mind as he placed this "art of suggestion" in the context of Japanese tradition.

There is a certain phase of Japanese painting … [in which] color and shading have been discarded in the eagerness of preserving the purity of the idea. It is not symbolism but infinite suggestiveness. … [T]he worship of the suggestive has been an integral part of our art-consciousness.

Indeed, in the same year Tenshin wrote a piece for the catalog of the "Taikan and Shunsō exhibition" held by the Century Association in New York in which he emphasized how deeply the two were connected to Japanese tradition. And in the speech given at the exposition of Saint Louis, he proudly describes the characteristics of Japanese painting born of Japanese soil:

[T]he development of painting in different countries has created different methods of approaching nature. … Art is no less an interpretation of nature than nature is a commentary on art. … The waves have become Korin to us as shadows have grown to be Rembrandt to you.

We must not be deceived by the word *mōrō*. Considering Shunsō's art anew from the perspective described by Tenshin, we notice that from an early date he was making extremely skillful use of distinctive materials like gold and silver, which no one would describe as vague or indistinct. If this is the Vague school, then the Vague school positively glitters.

(2014)

Travel, East and West

In February 2011, the Japanese Cultural Center in Paris hosted an international symposium on the theme "If there were no Shinkansen or TGV ..." (Si le Shinkansen et le TGV n'existaient pas ...). Setting out to compare the unique characteristics and achievements of Japan's Shinkansen and France's TGV (*train à grande vitesse*, "high-speed train"), the symposium was ultimately an exercise in comparative sociology and cultural studies using high-speed rail as a starting point.

France is justly proud of its rail technology. On the TGV Est line, trains travel faster than the Shinkansen, reaching speeds of up to 320 km/h (200 mph). For normal travel, this is the limit, but during test runs the TGV set a new world record by accelerating to more than 500 km/h (310 mph).

On the other hand, for sheer punctuality, the Shinkansen leaves not only France but all the countries of the West far behind. During rush hour at Tokyo station, there is a departure every three to five minutes. To the French, for so many trains to run almost exactly to schedule seems like a miracle—and it is all done on an extremely complicated timetable.

On France's Southeast Line, where TGV trains first saw service, trains run non-stop between Paris and Lyon, making the journey in around two hours. On the Tōkaidō Shinkansen line, too, the Nozomi travels from Tokyo to Nagoya in just under two hours, but it stops at many stations along the way. The Nozomi is the fastest train on the line, but there is also the Hikari, stopping at major stations, and the Kodama, stopping at every station. Since all three share the same tracks, a faster train often needs to pass a slower one, which in turn makes complex scheduling a necessity. Punctual operation is vital if this intricate timetable is to be followed without incident, and Japan's Shinkansen network achieves this difficult feat day after day with near-flawless precision.

The large number of trains in operation reflects the large number of people moving from place to place. In Japan, travel has been common since ancient times. Particularly during the extended peace of the Edo period, the roads were full of travelers, including women and children. The German doctor Engelbert Kaempfer, who accompanied the head of the Dutch factory at Nagasaki on his missions of tribute to Edo in the late seventeenth century, reported with admiration that not only were the highways kept extremely clean, they were "upon some days more crowded, than the publick streets in any the most populous town in Europe." As can be seen from the enormous popularity of Jippensha Ikku's picaresque novel *Shank's Mare* (*Tōkaidōchū hizakurige*), which relates the tale of a journey by foot along the Tōkaidō, even the common folk were remarkably casual about travel. Nor do they give the impression of spending much time on preparation; they appear to have set out on long journeys almost as if going for a walk. No doubt people did outfit themselves for travel to an extent, but equipment was minimal: the traditional hand and foot coverings, a staff, and a hat to keep the sun off. Very few of the travelers depicted in Hiroshige's *Fifty-three Stations of the Tōkaidō* are more heavily equipped than this.

This kind of travel was made possible by not only the relatively safety of the roads but also the well-equipped post stations (*shukuba*) along the way. Each station along the Tōkaidō offered a selection of lodgings ranging from luxury inns known as *honjin* to flophouses called *kichin yado*, as well as *toiyaba* where travelers could arrange to have people and luggage transported along the highway as necessary. Laborers, horses, palanquins—all were available for a fee. Travelers might send their luggage ahead to the next station or dispatch unnecessary items back to their homes, using the *toiyaba* much like the parcel delivery services of today. A nationwide travel and transportation network had been established.

In Europe, such things were unthinkable. War and conflict were always flaring up somewhere on the continent, and travelers were forced to go armed for their own protection. Even Goethe carried a pistol when he toured Italy in his youth. In the eighteenth century, it became common for the children of the English nobility to embark on the "Grand Tour" through Europe towards Italy once they had come of age, but these tourists were accompanied by crowds of servants bearing furniture and household goods. Travel guides of the time advised that bringing your own bedding with you was a must; if possible, it was best to bring a bed as well. This was a far cry from the nonchalance with which everyday Japanese people, including women and children, set out for popular destinations like the Ise Grand Shrine.

Japan's travel and accommodation network had developed to such a high level in large part due to the system of *sankin kōtai* or "alternate attendance" imposed by the Tokugawa shogunate. Daimyo from all over Japan were required to spend alternate years in their own domains and in Edo, meaning that vast numbers of people had to travel between these destinations every year— the "daimyo processions" depicted in the art and literature of the period.

Each daimyo had to travel with a retinue befitting the status of his house. For the average lord, this ranged from three to five hundred people, but representatives of the great clans like the Shimazu of Satsuma and the Maeda of so-called "million-*koku* Kaga" (a *koku* being defined as the amount of rice necessary to feed one person for one year) required a party of two or three thousand. Any number of large groups like this were traversing the highways at the same time, and each post station along each route had to be capable of meeting this peak demand.

The preparations required of the daimyo undertaking these journeys were also considerable. The first task was to fix the itinerary. A map of the various routes from Kanazawa to Edo survives from that period, and the itinerary it specifies combines so many roads that it looks like an *amidakuji* or "Ghost Leg" net with post stations as nodes. Depending on the route taken, the trip to Edo might take as few as ten days or as many as twelve. Road conditions and expected weather were all considered when selecting routes. The movements of other daimyo also had to be taken into account. As a general rule, the trip to or from Edo had to be made at the beginning of spring, meaning that three hundred lords and their retinues all shared the road at this time of year. If too many processions converged on the same post station, squabbles over the *honjin* and other disturbances tended to result, making this a situation to be avoided. The stations, for their part, were well aware of this, and careful not to double-book.

In this way, itineraries were decided with both travelers and inns making such allowances and preparations as were necessary well ahead of time. Once an itinerary was finalized and submitted to the shogunate, it could not be deviated from by a single day. Even if weather conditions or similar circumstances made the route unreasonable, it had to be followed. The unique ability of Japan's Shinkansen system to successfully execute a complicated predefined program of mass movement surely owes something to this history dating back to the Edo period.

France's TGV is not just high-speed but also long-distance rail, primarily connecting far-flung cities. But in Japan, major cities are connected by chains of medium-sized cities. Each of these smaller cities has its own unique character and becomes a node for travel in its own right. This level of urban continuity has defined Japan's unique national landscape for a long time, and it is difficult to find a contemporary European equivalent of the fifty-three stations of the Tōkaidō. The distance from station to station is generally between six and thirteen kilometers (roughly four to eight miles), with the shortest being less than two kilometers (just over a mile). Even with the occasional steep mountain path or other inconvenience, half a day's walk was usually sufficient to reach the next station. Moving at this leisurely pace, travelers would observe the natural world around them as it changed with the seasons, take in festivals and other events in the towns around the stations, and enjoy local delicacies.

Pilgrimages to the Ise Grand Shrine and other sacred sites were popular among the general populace as both spiritual journeys and sightseeing trips. To attract visitors, major shrines like the Ise Grand Shrine and Kotohiragū Shrine dispatched representatives—salesmen, essentially—known as *oshi* all across Japan. The role of the *oshi* included guidance along the way and preparations for worship, of course, but also extended to waiting on travelers at their lodgings and even organizing souvenirs. In this way they were not unlike modern-day travel agents. So-called leisure travel in Europe, however, did not truly take shape until the late nineteenth century after the expansion of the railroads, meaning that Japan was far ahead on this front.

From late 2011 to early 2012, the Suntory Museum of Art in Roppongi held an exhibition of Hiroshige's Tōkaidō ukiyo-e entitled *A Road Traveled by Feudal Lords and Pet Dogs*, featuring a complete set of both the Hōeidō *Fifty-three Stations of the Tōkaidō*, Hiroshige's breakthrough series, and the Reisho *Fifty-three Stations*, a later take on the subject inspired by the popularity of the first. I found myself savoring the fun of travel for the first time in a while, enjoying the scenery and customs of the stations along the way from Edo to Kyoto.

As it happens, the Hōeidō and Reisho editions were not the only *Fifty-three Stations* series Hiroshige created. The so-called *Gyōsho Tōkaidō* was also popular, as was the *Jinbutsu* ("Figure") *Tōkaidō* that focused on the travelers themselves. In all, Hiroshige completed more than twenty Tōkaidō-themed series. And, of course, he was not the only ukiyo-e artist to take up the theme. Hokusai, who Hiroshige considered his rival, produced his own version, as did Utamaro, Kunisada, Kuniyoshi, and Eisen. This list alone shows how popular travel was at the time, and this tradition of travel dating from the Edo period lives on vividly in the Shinkansen of today.

(2012)

Tokyo Station and the Culture of Travel

Tokyo Station's most notable structural characteristic is the sheer width of its façade—335 meters, or 1,100 feet. In formal terms, this feature can be considered a descendant of the late nineteenth century High Victorian Gothic style that the station's architect Tatsuno Kingo knew well, but even in the United Kingdom and other European countries with advanced rail systems, stations with a façade this wide are rare. (One exception is Amsterdam Centraal Station, which faces the harbor.) The reason for this is intimately tied up with the unique nature of Japanese and Western cities.

All the great cities of Western Europe, from London to Paris, Rome to Vienna, were once surrounded by walls. For the most part, these walls have long since been removed, but in the past they served as a boundary clearly separating the city's interior from the outside world. Railroads from one city to the next extended as far as these boundaries but did not enter the city proper. Transportation within the city was left to other systems, equivalent to the subways and bus routes of today. A city's train station was a dead end—a terminus—at the edge of that city. From the passengers' point of view, when they entered the station from the city, the tracks began before them and extended far into the distance straight ahead. This is the fundamental form of a terminus.

For example, in the case of Paris, the TGV departs from Part-Dieu Station in Lyon and proceeds through the stations of Paris Est, Paris Nord, Saint-Lazare, and Montparnasse, each of which faces the entrance to an old urban center. The lone exception was Orsay Station near the Louvre

Palace in central Paris, but this station was specially constructed to carry visitors to the Exposition Universelle in 1900; once the exposition was over, the line ceased operation and the station building was repurposed as the well-known Musée d'Orsay.

However, Tokyo Station was never intended as a terminus of this sort. In the 1886–1887 Ende–Böckmann proposal for a centralized government complex, "Central Station" (the working name for Tokyo Station at this point) occupied a crucial position as a way station. The Ende–Böckmann proposal was ultimately rejected, and, after much meandering, Tatsuno Kingo was commissioned as architect of "Central Station" in 1903. Nippon Railway wanted the new station to link Ueno Station, the entrance to Tokyo from the northeast, and Shinbashi Station (today's Shiodome Station), the point of departure for the Tōkaidō line heading southwest. In 1906, Nippon Railway was nationalized along with sixteen other private railway companies. When the Railway Authority was established two years later to oversee the rail business as a whole, the proposal for a central station connecting north and south was raised to the level of national policy. The common thread in all of these plans and proposals was the positioning of what would become Tokyo Station as a way station rather than a terminus.

What passengers see when they enter a way station from the front is quite unlike what they see in a terminus. Rather than receding into the distance straight ahead, the line extends from far left to far right. Naturally, the station building itself must reflect this difference. The tracks are the star of any railway system, and station architecture in any architectural

Tokyo Station at its opening.

style has a narrow rectangular plan—essentially a roof over the long platform and the segment of line where the train stops. At a terminal station,
one of the short sides of the building becomes the entrance facing the
city—the front of the station—but the face of the way station is one of its
long sides. This explains the remarkable, unparalleled width of Tokyo Station's façade.

The façades of European-style terminal stations tend to aim at a monu-
mental effect, with a high central tower, for example, or exaggerated ga-
bles. Many station buildings in the West have façades that soar to their
highest peak at the center. This may be a vestigial survival of the tradition
of cathedral architecture dating back to medieval times, in which the end
of the long nave in churches built on the Latin cross plan—the west-
work—was the magnificently ornamented "face" that the building presented to the city.

For a building as wide as Tokyo Station, however, that kind of cen-
ter-peaked design is impractical. Instead, Tatsuno placed a smaller trian-
gular-roofed main entrance at the center, and then balanced this with
domed rotundas at either end of the building to the left and right—a
highly ingenious solution.

The next problem, of course, is how to use this 335-meter-long façade
to best effect in urban planning. In order to view the building in its entirety, a wide space in front of it is the first requirement, and, to this end, the
Ende–Böckmann concept of a plaza in front of the station was revived in
slightly modified form. Alongside the ongoing restoration project for the
station building itself, plans are also afoot to reestablish the plaza in front

Postcard of Paris East Station,
early twentieth century.

235

of it. The goal is to preserve a relaxed atmosphere around the broad Gyōkō-dōri, which leads from the central entrance of the station to the Imperial Palace, by surrounding it with high-rise buildings. Meanwhile, around the Yaesu entrance on the opposite side of the station, the Tetsudō Kaikan, which blocked the view of the entrance, is to be torn down, and high-rise buildings erected to the south and north for a similar as around the central entrance. More than just an attempt to preserve the building itself, the restoration of Tokyo Station sparked a cascade of urban planning and development.

The nature of Tokyo Station thus had a decisive impact not only on the building's architecture but also on urban planning in Tokyo as a whole, and we can discern within it the traditional "culture of travel" in Japan dating back many centuries. Rail technology itself was imported from Europe, of course, but the application and operation of that technology on Japanese soil was shaped by long-standing traditions that remain vital today. In the age of the Shinkansen, this has become even more apparent.

In France's high-speed rail network, the eastbound line that departs from Paris Est Station is not connected to the Southeast Line departing from Part-Dieu Station in Lyon. In Japan, however, the Tōhoku, Jōetsu, Nagano, and Tōkaidō Shinkansen lines all meet at Tokyo Station, forming a network that extends as far as the Kyushu Shinkansen. When the current restoration project is complete, Tokyo Station will once more be a testament both to Japan's superb technological prowess and to the country's cultural heritage supported by deep-rooted tradition.

(2012)

Robots and Japanese Culture

In the latter half of the twentieth century, technological advances finally made the "machines that do the work of humans" or *robots* imagined some eighty years ago by Czech author Karel Ĉapek a reality. This included not just the humanoid robots popularly imagined as people with metal skin but a wide range of industrial robots with entirely different physical forms. Today, robots are active in countless fields. Some assist with large-scale factory manufacturing procedures, others care for the elderly and infirm, and some simply entertain in contests and competitions designed for their kind. The role of robots in our daily lives will only continue to grow.

All this raises a question: How should we think about the relationship between robots and humans—or, put more broadly, between humans and machines in general? The creation of robots required that full use be made of the fruits of technological civilization, which makes robots universal presences in that sense, crossing borders as easily as the other products of modern civilization. But how robots are used—perhaps more pointedly, how they are *treated*—depends on the country and people involved. We see differences grounded in the historical and cultural conditions of each individual region.

This question made its first and most vivid impression on me in the 1970s at an international symposium on the theme of technology and culture. The adoption of industrial robots had just begun to gather steam, with Japan in particular at the forefront and already seeing results. At the symposium, attendees from the Italian side proposed that one major factor impeding the implementation of robots was psychological resistance from workers; how, they asked, was Japan dealing with this problem? The question alone was sufficient to flummox the Japanese attendees. Uneasiness about the possibility of being replaced at work by a robot is understandable. This is a labor issue like any other, and calls for the exploration of measures to ensure that workers do not lose their jobs. But this "psychological resistance" spoken of by the Italians suggested that Italian workers rejected robots due to loathing of machines doing the work of people, or repulsion at the idea of the human domain being invaded by machines.

The Japanese side was not sure how to answer the Italians' question because, in Japan, there was no "psychological resistance" of this sort. Japanese workers not only accepted robots with no resistance at all, they gave them women's names like "Hanako" and "Momoe," treating them affectionately and even adorning them with ribbons. "Momoe" was the name of a popular singer at the time, and when the robot was not functioning as well as hoped, the workers would say things like "Momoe's out of sorts today." In other words, in Japan, robots were accepted immediately as co-workers and people.

Seeing Souls in Everyday Tools

The ready acceptance of robots in Japan is surely connected to the Japanese tendency, surviving since ancient times, to see not just animals and plants but also lifeless everyday tools as "sentient beings" with souls much like humans.

Consider the custom of *hari kuyō*, sometimes known in English as the Festival of Broken Needles and still widely practiced in Japan. At this annual event, sewing needles are thanked for their daily hard work by being carefully wrapped in paper to rest. Needles that are no longer needed are pushed into something soft like tofu or *konnyaku* jelly and entrusted to Shinto shrines. Similarly, "tombs" known as *fudezuka* for worn-out writing brushes can be seen at many shrines and temples around the country. Even to today's Japanese, needles and writing brushes are companions rather than lifeless tools; accordingly, when they are no longer needed, they are not simply discarded, but rather given an appropriate send-off with the same consideration that would be extended to a human.

The French term for "still life" is *nature morte*, "dead nature," but the traditional Japanese view of nature finds it so teeming with life that even frequently used tools like sewing needles and writing brushes become close companions and co-workers. Robots, which employ newer technology but are tools nonetheless, are no exception.

The sixteenth-century *Demons' Night Parade Picture-Scroll* (*Hyakki yagyō emaki*) depicts a parade of everyday objects, including parasols, musical instruments, and clothing, all trudging along like living things. A *hakama* (a kind of pleated skirt or pair of pants worn over a kimono) wriggles off its rack to join the parade, while a *koto* (thirteen-string zither) skitters along on newly sprouted legs instead of staying quietly indoors as usual: the depictions are both vaguely unsettling and somehow humorous, conveying a certain playfulness on the artist's part. What inspired that artist to paint this unusual parade scene was the idea that even these objects were living beings with their own wills and emotions. In the Edo period, there were many other bizarre monsters of this sort, like the *tōfu kozō* or "tofu boy" transformed from a block of tofu, but it is difficult to think of an equivalent in Western art history. In the world made by the Creator, there was a clear separation between humans and the rest of creation, and "dead nature" stayed dead.

Animism Meets High Technology

The gruesome depiction of hell in the right panel of Hieronymus Bosch's triptych *The Garden of Earthly Delights* (see plate 20) includes instruments such as a harp and trumpet. For this reason it is sometimes called the "Musical Hell," but the music played there was not pleasant. The instruments are painted as tools of torture employed on the sinners fallen into hell; the incongruity of using musical instruments in this way only heightens the horror. The writhing form of a sinner crucified on a harp speaks volumes about Bosch's fearsome imagination. Nevertheless, the harp is not torturing the sinner of its own volition. The instruments are nothing more than tools.

In the same way, when witches take to the sky on brooms in prints by Goya (not to mention many other paintings and stories), it is not the brooms that have the power to fly. A broom's flight is powered by the magic of the witch who rides it; without its witch, it would be just another object. If a broom were shown walking or flying on its own, like the parasol or *koto* in the *Demons' Night Parade Picture-Scroll*, the Western viewer would probably more readily view it as possessed by the witch than as a fellow creature in its own right. Once more we approach the "psychological resistance" felt by Italian workers towards robots.

The Japanese worldview, in which not just animals and plants but also inanimate objects are held to be alive, is usually called *animism*. It is thought to have been common worldwide in the distant past before being overwhelmed by the advance of civilization and subsequently lost. It is one of the unique characteristics of Japanese culture that this "animistic worldview" continues to thrive there, coexisting without any contradiction right alongside the most advanced technology. Indeed, Japan's robot developers devote a great deal of effort to robots that humans can empathize with and connect to emotionally, like Sony's AIBO, as well as the usual industrial robots to take on the work of humans.

Ĉapek coined the word *robot* based on the Czech word *robota*, meaning "forced labor"; as this fact makes abundantly clear, Western robots were beings made to take on painful, unpleasant work. For that reason, depictions of robots that had come to attain their own will usually posi-

Demons' Night Parade Picture-Scroll (*Hyakki yagyō emaki*) (details), Edo period. International Research Center for Japanese Studies. (See plate 21)

tioned them as antagonistic to humanity, like Hal in Stanley Kubrick's *2001: A Space Odyssey* or the androids of *The Matrix*. In Japan, however, imaginary robots were usually friendly, like Astro Boy and Doraemon. The head developer on Bandai's Doraemon Project, which aims to build a real-life Doraemon, describes the project's goal as creating "a robot that can not only walk around, but also communicate with humans and act as a friend one can trust and enjoy spending time with." Friendship between robots and humanity is, for the Japanese, a fundamental assumption.

Karakuri Ningyō As Technological Inheritance

Of course, to actually create robots, warm feelings about machinery alone are not enough. A high degree of technological prowess is required. Japan's importation of Western technological civilization and progress towards modernization proceeded rapidly beginning the Meiji period, but that success was partly due to a technological inheritance that had been accumulating in the previous centuries. When Westerners brought guns to Japan in the middle of the sixteenth century, the Japanese took to them quickly. Before long, they had learned to make their own weapons—indeed, some of the finest firearms in the world. This episode illustrates

both the strong curiosity the Japanese felt towards anything new and their extremely high level of technological sophistication.

Similarly, at around the same time, exquisite clocks were being made in Japan based on imported Western models. This went beyond imitation with the invention of Japanese clocks or *wadokei* which, uniquely in all the world, kept time using the temporal hour system. The temporal hour system, used by Japan in this period, takes the day from sunrise to sunset as a basic unit which is then subdivided. As a result, the exact length of each "hour" varies with the season and even from night to day—the hands of the clock must move at different speeds by day and by night. *Wadokei* that were able to make this changeover automatically were an astonishingly advanced technical achievement.

When the exquisite technology of *wadokei* was applied to the domain of play, the result was *karakuri ningyō* (literally "mechanical dolls") that can only be described as Edo-period robots. These automata were highly popular at the time, and some still survive here and there around Japan. By the end of the eighteenth century, publishers were even releasing technical works that described and illustrated their construction in detail. The best known *karakuri ningyō* was probably the Tea-Serving Doll (Chahakobi Ningyō). When a teacup was placed on the lacquered tray it bore, this doll would automatically begin walking towards the guest. When the guest took the cup from the tray, the doll would stop in its tracks. When the guest returned the cup to the tray, the doll would turn 180 degrees and return to its master. In other words, it was a robot, albeit a cute one, with an automatic control mechanism.

Interestingly, human automata were at the height of their European popularity in the eighteenth century as well. Jacques de Vaucanson's famous Flute Player no longer survives, but it was said to have played a repertoire of twelve songs by moving its fingers and tongue. In short, something that can only be called the prototype for the robot appeared in both Europe and Japan at almost the same time. One difference was that Vaucanson's Flute Player ran on springs and gears of steel; the springs in Japanese *karakuri ningyō* were made of whalebone, while gears and other components were generally made out of natural materials like wood and bamboo. This, too, was a uniquely Japanese characteristic.

In the last years of the Shogunate, Tanaka Hisashige, sometimes called "Karakuri Giemon" ("Giemon" having been his childhood name) delighted crowds with his Archer Boy (Yumihiki Dōji). After the Meiji Restoration, Tanaka founded a company known as Tanaka Engineering Works, which eventually evolved into the Toshiba Corporation. The technological flow of the Edo period continues unbroken today, and Japanese robotics was founded on a similar happy combination of high-level technological heritage and an animistic worldview in which tools and machines were seen as friends.

(2003)

Mount Fuji as World Cultural Heritage

The addition of Mount Fuji to UNESCO's World Heritage registry, and in particular its recognition as *cultural* heritage, has inspired much discussion. Reportedly, this was the first time the committee had accepted a natural phenomenon unmodified by the human hand into the "cultural" category. Japan's original application for cultural heritage status apparently simply used the title "Fujisan" (Japanese for "Mount Fuji"), but at the suggestion of the International Council on Monuments and Sites (ICOMOS), an advisory body to the World Heritage Committee which also surveyed the site in Japan, this was changed to "Fujisan, sacred place and source of artistic inspiration," the title under which the application for registry was ultimately approved.

The basic requirements for World Heritage recognition, natural or cultural, are uniqueness combined with "outstanding universal value." Thus, the addition of Mount Fuji to the registry represents new recognition that the belief system and artistic creations of the Japanese, both closely linked to Mount Fuji, have been recognized along with the Japanese psychology and aesthetic sensibility as both unique to Japan and a cultural inheritance to be shared by all humanity.

Praised by eighth-century *Man'yōshū* poet Yamabe no Akahito as "venerable, lofty, and noble, since the parting of heaven and earth," the unmistakable form of Mount Fuji—its peak rising above the clouds, its long, gentle lower slopes—has for centuries inspired not only awe and admiration but also belief in the divinity of the mountain itself. Tales are told of celestial maidens descending to its peak from the heavens and ancient dragon deities residing deep inside it. Takahashi no Mushimaro, a near-contemporary of Akahito whose works are also collected in the eight-century *Man'yōshū* anthology, called Mount Fuji "a god guarding the peace of Yamato, land of the rising sun," and he was neither first nor last to identify Mount Fuji itself as a deity.

Mount Fuji was also a living mountain, frequently smoking and sometimes erupting into flame, which can only have intensified its mystical image. When the author of the eleventh-century *Sarashina Diary* recalls passing close to Mount Fuji while traveling with her father from the eastern provinces to the central capital, she writes of her deep emotion at the sight, which "hardly seemed of this world." She also noted that "in the evening, fires could be seen rising" from the mountain. These flames were revered as divine, and Sengen Shrine was constructed to honor and worship the fire deity Asama. ("Sengen" is the Sino-Japanese pronunciation of the characters used to write "Asama.")

Starting in the late medieval period, Mount Fuji worship spread, and pilgrims began to visit and climb the mountain in greater numbers. Numerous "pilgrimage mandalas" (*sankei mandara*) were created, combining the functions of a map and a guidebook. As the name of the genre suggests, the climb was not undertaken for its own sake but rather as a pilgrimage, an act of faith. One such work from the late Muromachi period called the *Fuji Pilgrimage Mandala* (*Fuji sankei mandara*) is preserved at the Fujisan Hongū Sengen Taisha shrine near the mountain. Its lower half contains a sweeping depiction of the scenery at the base of the mountain, including the Miho Pine Grove (Miho no Matsubara), while Mount Fuji dominates its upper half, taller even than the solar and lunar discs in the sky. The mandala also contains intriguing and unmistakable depictions of people purifying themselves inside the grounds of Sengen Shrine before dressing in white and ascending to the peak in single file.

The mandala also depicts a triad of Buddhist deities at Mount Fuji's traditional "triple peak," and indeed the mountain was also sacred to Buddhism. There was a Buddhist temple dedicated to Mahāvairocana (Dainichi Nyorai) there which coexisted peacefully with Sengen Shrine until it was forced out by the Meiji government's Shinto–Buddhism Separation Order (*shinbutsu bunri rei*). This situation was not unique to Mount Fuji:

it was once common all over Japan to find Buddhist temples worshipped alongside the kami (gods) of Shinto on the grounds of Shinto shrines, just as Japanese people kept both miniature shrines and Buddhist altars in their home without thinking this peculiar in the least. This approach to religious belief, which would have been unthinkable in the West where worship of other gods was strictly forbidden, is highly Japanese, and Mount Fuji seems to embody it in some ways; calmly accepting its role in myth and legend, Buddhist teachings, and folk belief, the mountain makes no distinction between them as it towers far above.

Mount Fuji has provided the inspiration for artworks in a range of media, including literature, painting, crafts, and theater—further evidence of its cultural value. In the world of classical Japanese poetry (*waka*), the *Man'yōshū* contains many other poems praising the mountain in addition to the two cited above, and the mountain remains a popular theme to the present day, with some poets praising its beauty and others entrusting their own emotions to its form. Late in life, the twelfth-century poet Saigyō composed the poem that he is said to have been most satisfied with among his entire oeuvre:

kaze ni nabiku	like smoke from Fuji
Fuji no keburi no	drifting in the wind
sora ni kiete	and fading into sky
yukue mo shiranu	to parts unknown
waga omoi ka na	my own true feelings

This work evokes not only a Fuji to be gazed on with awe and respect, but also a closer, more approachable Fuji reflecting the poet's own feelings. Similar ideas are expressed in this *waka* by modern writer Wakayama Bokusui, a lifelong traveler and melancholy poet:

Fuji yo yuruse	O Fuji, forgive me
koyoi wa nan no	tonight, without any
yue mo nō	reason at all
namida hatenashi	my tears are boundless
nare o aogite	as I gaze up at you

Haiku poets, too, composed many masterpieces on the theme of Mount Fuji. One of the best-known examples is by Yosa Buson. Buson was also known for his paintings, including *Mount Fuji and Pines* (*Fugaku resshō-zu*), which depicts the mountain's dignified form rising above a series of pine groves in the foreground. This haiku explores similar imagery:

Fuji hitotsu	Fuji alone
uzumi nokoshite	left unburied—
wakaba kana	new leaves

(In the Japanese original, the word *Fuji* in the first line is actually written using the Chinese characters 不二, meaning "not two." This was a common alternate way to write the mountain's name, but the effect is that the line visually implies "Not-two alone," i.e. "Not-two one.")

One inheritor of Buson's fresh, painterly world, and in particular its serene coloristic expression, was Mizuhara Shūōshi. His haiku have a bracingly modern feel, and this one, written from Fujimi Kōgen, a site with a clear view of the mountain from Nagano a prefecture away, is particularly unforgettable:

Aofuji wa	Blue Fuji
tateri shirakaba mo	stands, the white birch
wakaba seri	has new leaves

Mount Fuji also appears in works of prose, from the "forefather of tales" (i.e., of the Japanese *monogatari* genre), the *Tale of the Bamboo Cutter*, to the *Tales of Ise*, the *Tale of the Soga Brothers*, and many other stories, fables, and, eventually, novels. Illustrations of scenes from these works inspired paintings, handcrafts, and eventually colorful sets for Noh and kabuki plays, a fact which speaks eloquently to the enormous power of Mount Fuji as a source of artistic inspiration.

In the field of painting, the earliest surviving depiction of Mount Fuji is in the *Illustrated Biography of Prince Shōtoku* in the Hōryūji Treasures Hall of the Tokyo National Museum. Dating from the middle of the eleventh century, the painting is based on the legend of Prince Shōtoku's cross-ing Mount Fuji on a black horse from Kai Province. Countless painters since then have tried their hand at depicting the sacred mountain, not least the master painter Sesshū. In the Edo period in particular, the imprint on the public consciousness left by the Mount Fuji imagery of ukiyo-e artists like Hokusai and Hiroshige should not be overlooked. As is well known, when works like Hokusai's *Thirty-six Views of Mount Fuji* (*Fugaku sanjū rokkei*) and Hiroshige's *One Hundred Famous Views of Edo* (*Meisho Edo hyakkei*) found their way to Europe in the second half of the nineteenth century, they were enormously influential on artists like Whistler, Monet, Van Gogh, and Bonnard, and the *japonisme* movement generally. Nor was this influence limited to painters; stimulated by "The Great Wave off Kanagawa" (Kanagawa oki nami ura) in Hokusai's *Thirty-six Views*, sculp-

Hata no Chitei, *Illustrated Biography of Prince Shōtoku* (*Shōtoku Taishi eden*), 1069. Tokyo National Museum.

Sesshū (attributed), *Mount Fuji and Seikenji Temple* (*Fuji Seikenji-zu*), sixteenth century.
Eisei Bunko Museum.

tor Camille Claudel created *The Wave* (*La Vague*), and when the composer
Debussy was working on his symphonic poem *The Sea* (*La Mer*), a copy of
the same work was hanging in his studio. The first edition of the sheet music for *The Sea* even featured Hokusai's print on its cover.

And that was not all. Call it the power of art, but long before the age of
japonisme, during the period of close relations with China, Japanese art
not only played a role in conveying Japan's unique, refined aesthetic sensibility to foreign audiences, pictures of Mount Fuji in particular had the effect of cultivating interest in and admiration for Japan itself. The ink-wash
painting *Mount Fuji and Seikenji Temple*, said to be the work of Sesshū, is
one example. In this work, which is wider than it is tall, the Miho Pine
Grove is to the right and the venerable temple Seikenji to the left. A palely
shining Mount Fuji rises above both, slightly left of center. The superb
composition of this masterpiece has been copied by any number of painters since, but what is most interesting is the comment written on the
painting by the Ming-dynasty literatus Zhan Zhonghe, who expresses his
desire to one day travel to Japan himself, gaze up at Fuji, and steal the
feathered mantle from a celestial maiden in the Miho Pine Grove.

In the twentieth century, the French dancer Hélène Giuglaris became
fascinated by Noh, and even during the Second World War kept up her
studies of the form despite the great difficulty inherent in doing so. After
the war was over, her performance of *The Feathered Robe* (*Hagoromo*) at the

Guimet Museum received rave reviews from critics. Giuglaris hoped fervently to dance the same piece in the Miho Pine Grove one day, but this was not to be: before long, she collapsed during a performance, just at the scene where the celestial maiden departs our world, and her short life came to an end at the young age of thirty-five. She reportedly had leukemia. Today, there is a monument at the pine grove in Giuglaris's memory, erected by her husband and containing a lock of her hair.

Focus of religious faith, source of artistic inspiration: Mount Fuji without question deserves its place among the world's cultural heritage.

(2013)

Afterword

I. Word and Image: The Japanese Aesthetic Consciousness

This chapter is based on an April 2014 lecture for employees of Shizuoka Prefecture delivered at the invitation of the prefectural governor, although many of the visual aids from the original lecture could not be included.

II. Japanese Beauty, Western Beauty

"East Meets West: Forms of Expression in Japanese and Western Art" was the keynote speech of the Comité International d'Histoire de l'Art's September 1991 Tokyo Colloquium, "Japan and Europe in Art History." The speech was originally delivered in English.

"The Dawn of Japanese Oil Painting" was first published in issue 1382 of the art magazine *Flower of the Nation* (*Kokka*). "Sentiment and Sensibility: Beneath the Surface of *Wasei Yuga*" was published in the catalog for *Wasei Yuga: Orbits of Creativity*, an exhibition held at the Ōhara Museum of Art from December 2003 to February 2004. This was the first appearance of the word *wasei yuga* ("Japan-made oil paintings").

"Japan and the West in the Art of Takeuchi Seihō" was published in the catalog for *Celebrating 150 Years since the Birth of Takeuchi Seihō*, an exhibition held at the Umi-Mori Art Museum from November to December 2014.

III. Roots of the Japanese Aesthetic Consciousness

"Word and Image," "Chinese Characters and the Japanese Language," "The Aesthetics of the Margin," "Postcards and Place," "*Gagaku* Without *Gagaku*," "Canonical Beauty and Situational Beauty," "Taikan and Fuji," "Whither *Passing Spring*?" "School Songs and Musical Education," "Fukuzawa Yukichi, Traditionalist," "Blossoms of Devotion: Goshun, Buson, and the White Plum," "Dragons, Tigers, and Museums," "Interpretation as Transformation," "Interpretation as Creative Act," "The Glittering Vague," "Travel, East and West," and "Mount Fuji as World Cultural Heritage" were originally published in the magazines *Asteion* and *Discovery* (*Daikōkai*). "The Culture of Name Succession" was originally published in the *Kyoto Shimbun*. "Bridges and the Japanese" was originally published in the magazine *Bungeishunjū*.

"Tokyo Station and the Culture of Travel" was included in *Tokyo Station Marunouchi Building: Preservation and Restoration*, a collection published in 2011.

"Robots and Japanese Culture" was an essay originally published in French in the catalog for *Fantaisies cybernétiques*, an exhibition held at the Maison de la culture du Japon à Paris in October 2003.

I would like to express my gratitude to all the organizations, facilities, and publications that originally offered me a platform for these lectures and writings. And I would also like to express my heartfelt thanks to Chikuma-shobō, and particularly my editor Ōyama Etsuko, for taking on the project of publishing this book.

Takashina Shūji
August 2015

Original Publication Details

I. Word and Image: The Japanese Aesthetic Consciousness

Word and Image: The Japanese Aesthetic Consciousness (Kotoba to imēji: Nihonjin no biishiki)
> Heavily edited version of lecture delivered in Shizuoka Prefecture, 2014.

II. Japanese Beauty, Western Beauty

East Meets West: Forms of Expression in Japanese and Western Art (Higashi to nishi no deai: Nihon oyobi seiyō no kaiga ni okeru hyōgen yōshiki ni tsuite no shomondai)
> In *Bijutsushi ni okeru Nihon to seiyō: Kokusai bijutsushi gakkai Tōkyō kaigi 1991*. Tokyo: Chūōkōron Bijutsu Shuppan, 1995.

The Dawn of Japanese Oil Painting (Wasei yuga-ron)
> *Kokka* vol. 1382 (Dec. 20, 2010). Asahi Shimbun Shuppan.

Sentiment and Sensibility: Beneath the Surface of *Wasei Yuga* (Kansei to jōnen: "Wasei yuga" o sasaeta mono)
> Ōhara Bijutsukan/Kotohiragū daiikkai bunka kōryū ten, 2003.
> *Wasei yuga: Sozō no kiseki* (catalog).

Japan and the West in the Art of Takeuchi Seihō (Seihō geijutsu ni okeru Seiō to Nihon)
> Umi-Mori Art Museum, 2014. *Seitan 150 nen kinen: Takeuchi Seihō* (catalog).

III. Roots of the Japanese Aesthetic Consciousness

Word and Image (E to moji)
> *Asteion* vol. 61 (Nov. 25, 2004). Suntory Bunka Zaidan/Asteion Henshū Iinkai.

Chinese Characters and the Japanese Language (Kanji to Nihongo)
> *Asteion* vol. 62 (Apr. 29, 2005).

The Culture of Name Succession (Shūmei no bunka)
"Gendai no kotoba," *Kyoto Shimbun*, Oct. 31, 2005.

The Aesthetics of the Margin (Yohaku no bigaku)
Asteion vol. 64 (May 1, 2006).

Postcards and Place (Meisho ehagaki)
Asteion vol. 65 (Nov. 1, 2006).

Gagaku Without *Gagaku* (Ukeirerarenakatta gagaku)
Daikōkai vol. 63 (Jul. 2007).

Canonical Beauty and Situational Beauty (Jittai no bi to jōkyō no bi)
Asteion vol. 67 (Nov. 29, 2007).

Taikan and Fuji (Taikan to Fuji)
Asteion vol. 68 (Apr. 26, 2008).

Whither *Passing Spring*? ("Yuku haru" no yukue)
Asteion vol. 69 (Oct. 24, 2008).

School Songs and Musical Education (Shōga to ongaku kyōiku)
Daikōkai vol. 69 (Jan. 2009).

Fukuzawa Yukichi, Traditionalist (Dentōshugisha Fukuzawa Yukichi)
Asteion vol. 70 (Apr. 24, 2009).

Blossoms of Devotion: Goshun, Buson, and the White Plum
(Hakubai ni takusu omoi)
Asteion vol. 72 (Apr. 28, 2010).

Dragons, Tigers, and Museums (Ryū, tora, soshite bijutsukan)
Asteion vol. 73 (Oct. 29, 2010).

Interpretation as Transformation (Kaishaku wa sakuhin no sugata o kaeru)
Asteion vol. 74 (Apr. 28, 2011).

Interpretation as Creative Act (Sōzō kōi toshite no kaishaku)
Asteion vol. 75 (Oct. 28, 2011).

Bridges and the Japanese (Nihonjin to hashi)
Bungeishunjū (Sep. 1998 special edition).

The Glittering Vague (Kirameku mōrōtai)
Asteion vol. 81 (Nov. 13, 2014).

Travel, East and West (Tabi no tōzai)
Asteion vol. 76 (May 11, 2012).

Tokyo Station and the Culture of Travel (Tōkyō eki to tabi no bunka)
Tōkyō Marunouchi ekisha: Hozon/fukugen (catalog), 2012.

Robots and Japanese Culture (Robotto to Nihon bunka)
Maison de la culture du Japon à Paris, 2003. *Fantaisies cybernétiques* (catalog).

Mount Fuji as World Cultural Heritage (Sekai bunka isan toshite no Fuji-san)
Asteion vol. 79 (Nov. 21, 2013).

About the Author

Takashina Shūji was born in 1932 in Tokyo. After graduating from the University of Tokyo's College of Arts and Sciences, he studied in France from 1954 to 1959 on the invitation of the French government. Since his return to Japan, he has held positions including professor at the University of Tokyo, director general of the National Museum of Western Art, and his current role as director of the Ōhara Museum of Art. A specialist in Western art from the Renaissance onwards, he is also deeply versed in the art of Japan. His many publications include *Light and Dark in the Renaissance* (*Runessansu no hikari to yami*, recipient of the Minister of Education's Art Encouragement Prize), *A History of Modern Art in Japan* (*Nihon kindai bijutsushiron*), *Van Gogh's Eye* (*Gohho no me*), *A History of French Painting* (*Furansu kaigashi*), *Picasso: The Logic of Plagiarism* (*Pikaso: Hyōsetsu no ronri*), *Twentieth-Century Art* (*Nijusseiki bijutsu*), *A History of Modern Painting* (*Kindai kaigashi*, in two volumes), and *The Patrons of Art* (*Geijutsu no patorontachi*). His other contributions to the Japanese art world include translations of works by Edgar Wind and Kenneth Clark.

About the Translator

Matt Treyvaud is an Australian-born literary translator who lives south of Tokyo. His recent translations include Natsume Sōseki's *Ten Nights Dreaming* and Toh EnJoe's *The Squirrel Awakes*.

〈英文版〉日本人にとって美しさとは何か
The Japanese Sense of Beauty

2018年3月27日　第1刷発行

著　者　高階 秀爾
訳　者　マット・トライヴォー
発行所　一般財団法人 出版文化産業振興財団
　　　　〒101-0051 東京都千代田区神田神保町3-12-3
　　　　電話　03-5211-7282（代）
　　　　ホームページ　http://www.jpic.or.jp/

印刷・製本所　大日本印刷株式会社